the daria™

by Peggy Nicoll

MTV BOOKS

POCKET BOOKS

Writer: Peggy Nicoll
Editor: Michele Tomasik
Art Director/MTV: Karen Hyden
Art Direction/Reiner Design: Roger Gorman and Leah Sherman
Art Production Manager: Bryon Moore
Production Manager: Sara Duffy
Production Assistants: Patrick Intrieri, Christine Dekhi, Laura Murphy
Artists: Aaron Augenblick, Anthony Davis, Kirk Albert Etienne, George Fort, Guy Moore, Olivia Ward, Natalia Zurabova
Color Supervisor: Olivia Ward
Color Designers: Michael Cavallaro, Chris Costan, Laura Margulies, Amy Melson

Daria Creative Supervisors: Glenn Eichler, Susie Lewis Lynn

Special Thanks at MTV: Eduardo A. Braniff, Cindy Brolsma, Avery Cobern, Janine Gallant, Julie Johns, Andrea Labate, George Lentino, Kim Noone, Robin Silverman, Donald Silvey, Machi Tantillo, Abby Terkuhle, Van Toffler

Special thanks at Pocket Books to: Brian Blatz, Gina Centrello, Twisne Fan, Lisa Feuer, Max Greenhut, Donna O'Neill, Liate Stehlik, and Kara Welsh. Also thanks to Greg Wade at Color Associates.

An Original Publication of MTV Books/Pocket Books

books

POCKET BOOKS, a division of Simon and Schuster, Inc.
1230 Avenue of the Americas, New York NY 10020

ISBN: 0-671-02596-1

First MTV Books/Pocket Books trade paperback printing November 1998

10 9 8 7 6 5 4 3 2 1

Printed in the U.S.A.

MIDDLETON MUSINGS/ WINTER

'72

Celebrating his eleventh year as a snowboard instructor in Winter Park, Colorado, **Lad Duncan** writes: "Hi! Are you?" Lad wants you all to know that the "powder's bitchin'" and that his son's moved out so it's safe to come on down....L.A. transplant **Marjorie Kurtis** says she's given up her acting/food management careers to become a writer. In her first self-published book, *The Art of Acting*, Marjorie gives an insider's view on how to make it to the top....**Jake** and **Helen (Barksdale) Morgendorffer** recently held a big bash for their twenty-third wedding anniversary. Helen wants those who attended to know that daughter Daria is feeling much better and is back to her cheerful self. "She had the flu, which sapped her energy and made her a little sarcastic." Helen also adds that Daria's sister, Quinn, was just joking when she said her biggest fear in life is to have an ugly child. "It's that Morgendorffer wit!" Helen swears she'll make the next reunion and Jake writes: "Hey, if anyone needs some first-rate marketing consulting, I'll give you the old college discount!"...Congratulations to **Nancy "Woodsy" Woods** for passing the bar. Nancy graduated from Middleton Law in '79 and plans to practice in Sunvale.... If you're in the Santa Fe area, make sure to visit **Doug Preston** behind the counter at Turquoise and Trinkets...

RapidTransmit from DariaM

I want to keep track of my classmates after graduation, so I'm planning to have them branded.

Send | Print

Bb Baby-sitting Spreadsheet, Quinn's

Waif

Name/Kid	Phone	Television
Elliots Parker, Wick 9-month twins Cute. If they inherit their father's looks.	900 accessible Conference calling Call-forwarding Call-waiting	Satellite No V-Chip Big screen Bulky remote
Hanlons Julia, 9 Katherine, 12 Proof that you're never too young for highlighting!	Call-waiting *69	Cable Average-size screen (Julia insists on watching figure skating. Could those outfits be any tackier? And what's with the frosted shadow?)
Greens Todd, 8 Walks funny and has a really round head.	Not cordless–is that legal? And gross sticky stuff on the part you hold with your hand.	No cable!!! Okay home-movie selection, though.
Mr. O'Conner Jackie, 7 Really cute and smart. Always asking me where I got my clothes.	900 accessible Call-waiting Three lines! Caller I.D. display!	Big screen Screen within screen (watch music videos AND Fashionvision although difficult to follow both at same time) Satellite dish Surround sound
Philips Jonathan, 6 months Too much of a crybaby	Long-distance block No call-waiting!!	Small screen hidden away in depressing family room. Perfectly good shelf space cluttered by books.

RapidTransmit from DariaM

```
It takes a village to watch my sister
watch a child.
```

Send   Print

House	Food	Notes	Rating
Spanish; wear earth tones. Swimming pool (heated) Makeup mirror in bathroom. Complete view of driveway from house; back-door escape route.	Soda (diet and non) Square chips Round chips Ridged chips Salsa Barbecue Chips Tortilla chips Onion dip	Babies, diapers: bad. Can't tell parents about pool parties: good.	Four smileys
All-white furniture makes spills difficult to conceal–do not invite Jeffy over. Wear warm colors for good contrast.	Soda (no diet) Baby-sitter "plate" of vegetables and fruit is insulting. Found dessert with crunchy top hidden in vegetable bin.	Katherine's sweet, but she kept asking me stupid questions like how a light-bulb works. I explained the "off" and "on" switch to her and then she just walked away.	Pass, unless Mom's having her Successful Women's Support Group over.
Only Daria's clothes would go with such dumpy furniture. Unattractive dog.	Beef sticks and other unpopular people food. Gross meat loaf and cheap grape ice cream hidden in locked garage fridge–like I would touch that!	Demon child Todd kept trying to make me play games with him. Finally agreed to hide-and-seek, then went back to *Pretty Woman.*	Already had their number blocked. See about having Stacy put on FC probation for referring me.
Super modern! Leather furniture goes with everything except my suede clogs. Switches control lighting, music; automated driveway gate–have friends park down street.	The best! Mr. O'Conner calls me that morning to stock up on my favorites!	Jackie wouldn't go to bed until I told her the fashion monster would come after her and turn her clothes into polyester. She's so cute!	Five smileys! Mr. O'Conner is so nice! He's even asked me to go sailing with him!
Colonial Furniture really old and what's with hanging carpets on walls? No bright colors or T-shirts with slogans.	Surprisingly good, although not sure if Joey should have eaten that rum cake. Hope he got home all right.	Vent from Jonathan's room connected to family room, so we had to listen to him crying all night.	One smiley. Gave them Sandi's number.

Bb Budgets, Weekly Discretionary Income

JAKE

$20 Quinn's allowance

$25 Daria's allowance

$36 Model boat kit

$28 Two rounds of beer at the Rathskeller for the guys

$3.50 Matinee "Gimme Shelter."

$10 Beer, waiting for the guys to show up and pay me back. Jerks.

$69 Racing form, bets ("Damnation" sucks!), lunch at Horseplay Café

$3.50 Matinee "Shaft."

$.79 Gum

QUINN

$3.50 "Happy Rainbow" nail decals

$5 Ocean Blue scrunchy (although it looks more like Sky Blue)

$10 Earrings for Sandi's birthday present (based on estimate of what she spent on my present)

$15 For Daria to tell my date she's a foreign-exchange student

$7.50 "Happy Rainbow" nail-decal remover

$6 True Blue scrunchy in velveteen

$8 Sheer orange scarf (note: Don't use as lamp-shade decoration this time)

$18 More reprints of school pictures (see if Mom will reimburse)

$4 Green Scrunchy

Notes: Short again!
Wear halter top to dinner.

RapidTransmit from DariaM

A penny saved isn't worth a dime.

Send   Print

HELEN

$20	Quinn's allowance
$25	Daria's allowance
$45	"Making Friends for Fun & Profit" power breakfast
$60	Retouch head shot for press events
$70	Birthday present for Rita (ask Marianne what I bought)
$25	Contribution to "No Means No!" Women's Rights Fund
$10	Negotiation Strategies on Tape: "No Is Not an Answer"
$20	Daria (she loses that ammo belt or else)
$95	Dinner with Michele Landon (note: Discreetly call next week re: committee opening)
$20	Quinn (she loses that halter top or else)
$30	Breakfast seminar "Breaking Up Is Profitable to Do—Is Divorce Law for You?"
$26	Book—"The Sensuous Executive: How to Schedule Sex & More!"

DARIA

$5	Pizza
$15	Mr. Fun's World of Games
$45	Montana cabin fund

Cc Canberra, E-mail from Daria

To: Nic@DownUnder

From: DariaM

Subject: Satellite Dish

Dear Nicole,

Yes, it's true. High school in America is every bit as exciting and glamorous as what you see on TV. Just yesterday Brittany (she's a cheerleader—that's an American term for "brain-damaged") woke half the class when she got a piece of gum stuck in her part. I offered to dissolve it with some of the sulfuric acid I've been stockpiling, but her boyfriend, Kevin, who loves her very much, wouldn't allow it. He was afraid it might change her hair color.

The academic program here is rigorous. If you don't know how to throw a football, they make you take tests and write papers. Last week we had to write about current events. Mr. O'Neill liked my essay "Do We Really Need an Ozone Layer?" so much, he's invited my mother to school to discuss it. All this excitement is killing me. Very, very slowly.

Don't worry about Americans judging you on your criminal ancestry. Most people here know very little about Australia except that it's in Europe somewhere. In point of fact, Australia is so far away that you may never get any visitors from Lawndale.

Hey. Would it be very hard for me to get an Australian green card?

Daria

RapidTransmit from DariaM

I'd move to Australia after high school, but it's too close to home.

Send | Print

Cc Cheerleader Etiquette

CHEERLEADERSHIP! THE ENTHUSIAST'S GUIDE TO SCHOOL SPIRIT!

DO'S
AND
DON'TS!

Whenever we're at a big game, we know that all eyes are on us. But what many of us forget is that people look to us for Leadership and Guidance off the field as well! So I say, as Cheerleaders, let's not let our fans down! Right?! Right!!

Yes!

Tell Kevin to buy costumes early this year!!!

Here are a few Do's and Don'ts:

DO keep neatly Groomed all day long!

Of course you're really cute and pretty—you wouldn't be a Cheerleader if you weren't! But that doesn't mean you can go to school with, say, your Hair all staticky-clingy. I mean, you wouldn't expect your Boyfriend to come to school in a Dress, would you? Unless it was Halloween or something, and they were all out of costumes at the store, and he couldn't think of anything else, and even then. Always check your Hair and Makeup between classes, including hard-to-see spots like the back of your Ponytail because you have to look good coming *and* going!

Check rearview mirror in car before school and after lunch.

DON'T look Sad!!!

Cheerleaders are supposed to be "Cheer-y!" so keep Smiling at all times. If the teacher starts talking about something really Depressing like a war or plague or something, just pretend he or she is describing a movie and picture the Happy Ending in your head!

Everyone wins the war and goes to a great big party to dance!

DO date athletes!

While it's okay to date civilians if they're really cute and have really cool Cars, your Public kind of expects you to date the Captain of the Basketball Team or the QB. Besides, it's easier to date jocks because when they have Practice, *you* have Practice, and you both have to be at the same Games at the same Time so it makes planning stuff a whole lot easier. And if you break up, you can always get even with Him by Flirting with Other Guys between cheers.

I never thought of that!

Good thinking!

DON'T yell off the court or field!!!

Sometimes you're so used to Cheering, you forget not to Yell in normal conversations. This is a toughie. One Cheerleader I know used to stand in the back of the classroom so her Voice wouldn't sound as loud in case she forgot. I don't recommend this because you may have to squint to see the Cute Guys in the front of the class, and that can cause Wrinkles. Better to always wait at least five Seconds before answering any questions so you have time to orient Yourself.

Is that one, two, three, or one Missisipi, two Missisipi, three Missisipi?

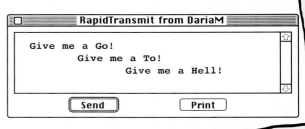

RapidTransmit from DariaM

Give me a Go!
Give me a To!
Give me a Hell!

Send   Print

Stacy, here is the Chez Pierre menu I promised you. I pointed out some of the things that are really nice and really foreign. Please return when you're done studying, and good luck with Seth!!!

Chez Pierre
Subtle lighting enhances your youthfu skin tone but may make guy look even cuter than he is.
Marie Antoinette. Gave everyone dessert or something.
MARIE ANTOINETTE
Louis the, um, who cares. French clothing is much cuter now!
Soda looks so elegant in these.
Jean Paul—guys' names sound so much better in French!
Lots of silverware so you can pick and choose. And the napkins—swans!!!
Velvet chairs so clothes don't wrinkle.

Tables far enough apart so you don't have to look at anyone unattractive.

Chez Pierre

CHEZ PIERRE LES ENTRÉES

MEDAILLONS DE BŒUF BÉARNAISE $32

(Rhymes with: Doof "Brrr"-says)
(the good kind of beef with yellow sauce)

ENTRECÔTE DU BŒUF AUX CHAMPIGNONS SAUVAGES $22

(Rhymes with: Zent-never mind. Besides, cheapest thing on menu so forget it)

ESCALOPE DE VEAU $26

(Rhymes with: Floppy day Moo)
(scallops—too fishy)

BOUILLABAISSE $28

(Rhymes with: Julie in Lace)
(just soup)

FILET DE PORC $24

(Rhymes with: Delay day Fork)
(pork chops-but you have to ask for applesauce;
cheap, so order an appetizer, I mean orderve)

Helpful phrases:

Waiter, my soda is flat. Send it back.
Garson, mon soda est flat. Envoyer il revenir.

The bouillabaisse is too fishy. Send it back.
Le bouillabaisse est trop fishy. Envoyer il revenir.

Water-l'eau
Bread-le pain
Soda-soda
Artificial sweetener-l'Equal

Cc Crests, Jane's Drawings of

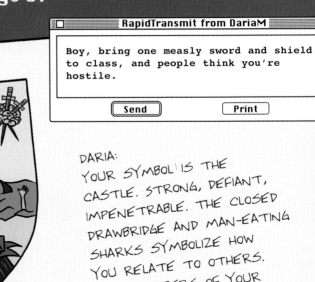

RapidTransmit from DariaM

Boy, bring one measly sword and shield to class, and people think you're hostile.

Send | Print

NE PLUS ULTRA

DARIA:
YOUR SYMBOL IS THE CASTLE. STRONG, DEFIANT, IMPENETRABLE. THE CLOSED DRAWBRIDGE AND MAN-EATING SHARKS SYMBOLIZE HOW YOU RELATE TO OTHERS. THE MEMBERS OF YOUR IMMEDIATE FAMILY ARE REPRESENTED BY THE SWORDS PIERCING YOUR BRAIN.

I HAVE CHOSEN INVERTED JOCKS PLUNGING TO THE DEPTHS OF THE OCEAN TO REPRESENT THE DEATH OF STUPIDITY. BELOW, PILLOWS SYMBOLIZE ULTIMATE STATE ATTAINABLE BY ANY TEEN: SLEEP. THE CHEETAH DEVOURING A SMALL, HELPLESS ANIMAL IS ME. CAN WE GET SOME PIZZA AFTER SCHOOL? I'M STARVING.

I HAVE A DREAM

Dd Daria's Excuses

DATE/IMPOSER	EVENT	REASON/EXCUSE	REACTION	NOTES
11/11 Mom	Cousin's wedding	CO/"I'm afraid I'd be so overcome with joy I'd have to shoot myself, and you know how hard it is to get blood out of taffeta."	Offered me twenty dollars; got it up to fifty.	Don't forget reading materials.
11/14 Mr. O'Neill	Tutor Kevin	CO/IW/"Good idea. Let's see Kevin ignore all my phone calls and letters now!"	"Come to think of it, I already asked Jodie."	Reusable with other faculty.
12/18 Mom	Clean room for Grandmother's visit	RB/"Tell Grandma the right side of the mattress is the dry side."	Didn't work, but Quinn had dinner in her room for three nights straight.	In future, remember: wet-mattress line no deterrent to incontinent visitor.
3/10 Mom	Company picnic	CO, RB/"I have a date."	"We're leaving at noon."	Next time use a believable excuse.
3/16 Dad	Pass the television guide	RM/"I can't lift things. Remember? The accident?"	"Oh...right."	Make sure no one else is around when using this one.
5/22 Mom	Remove trip wire from room	RM/"But somebody might get hurt."	Took scalpel from nightstand and cut wire.	Consider loosening door hinges.
6/1 Mom	Family island vacation	CO, CQ, IW, RR, RB/ "I have a fear of landing."	"Then we'll just have to go to family counseling until you're cured."	Damn it, she got me.

Codes:

CO—Would involve contact with others
CQ—Would involve contact with Quinn
IW—Would interfere with crossword puzzle, video game, tile counting, sleep
RR—Would require leaving room
RB—Would require leaving bed
RM—Would require moving

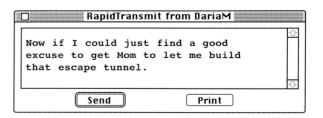

RapidTransmit from DariaM

Now if I could just find a good excuse to get Mom to let me build that escape tunnel.

Send Print

Ee E-mail, Important

TO: Brittany!!!
FROM: Nospmot

Hey Babe,
Pretty cool now that we're on-line. My email name is Nospmot. That's my last name spelled in reverse without the "h." I thought Nospmot would be easier to remember than Nospmoht.

Sorry about your sweater. Next time we'll find a place that isn't so grassy. Like tomorrow night?

Email me, babe

Nospmot

TO: Kevvy
FROM: Brittany!!!

Hi, Kevvy,
T-h-o-m-p-s-o-n
Nospmo—whatever, it's hard to remember, so I'll just use Kevvy, okay? Don't worry about the grass stains. Next time I'll make sure to wear dark colors or maybe we should just stay in the car, although we have to be more careful about where we park 'cause last time that old guy really creeped me out. Tomorrow night sounds great!

Brittany!!!
P.S. Brian showed me how to scan in a picture of me! How do you like it?

TO: Brittany!!!
FROM: Kevvy

Dear Brittany,
Since we're not going to see each other until tomorrow, how about if we play a little game tonight? Let's call it "our last date." Tell me, Brittany, in rich detail, how we got the grass stains on your sweater. Don't leave out anything…touch, feel, scents. Also, do you have any other pictures that are a little more, you know, "personal"?

Love,
Kevvy

TO: Kevvy
FROM: Brittany!!!

Dear Kevvy,
I can't believe you don't remember how we got the grass stains! I mean, check out that scratch mark on your back–maybe THAT will make your memory jog! Wait a minute….you weren't drinking or anything were you? 'Cause you know how I feel about that!

Brittany!!!
P.S. I sent you a new picture even though you don't deserve it.

TO: Brittany!!!
FROM: Kevvy

Dear Brittany,
Of course I remember how we got the stains! How could I forget, my love? I just want to relive the precious moments in all their splendor, through YOUR words. So start from the beginning…how we were lying next to each other, how I took you in my arms, what you called out in the throes of passion. Spare no detail!

Yours forever,
Kevvy
P.S. I looove that new picture. I only wish the bikini didn't hide all your natural beauty. Could you send me one just a little more revealing? For me? Please?

TO: Brittany!!!
FROM: Nospmot

Hey Babe,
You're supposed to email me back! I said I was sorry about the sweater!

Nospmot

RapidTransmit from DariaM

The Web offers complete anonymity, especially when you can't remember your own name.

Send Print

TO: Kevvy
FROM: Brittany!!!

Dear Kevvy,
Gee, Kevvy. I don't know if I can talk about THAT in email. I mean, what if someone else read it? It would be so embarrassing! And I heard somewhere about these computer people who can spy on your mail and tell your boss, not that we have a boss, but if we did, we could be in big trouble.

Do you think dreams come true? 'Cause I dreamt last night that I got mud all over my new suede heels (the ones from Cashman's), and I really hope that doesn't happen.

Love,
Brittany!!!
P.S. I already told you, I'm not mad about the sweater!

TO: Brittany!!!
FROM: Kevvy

Dear Brittany!!!
Tell me about the heels. How high are they? Do they come to a nice, sharp stiletto point and do they have a little strap around your silken ankle? Are they easy to slip off so I can caress the long, soft curves of your legs? Tell me about them, Brittany. And tell me about the short little micro-mini and the lacy teddy you'll be wearing with them. I want to know everything....

I love you,
Kevin
P.S. I'm still waiting for that sexy picture!

TO: Brittany!!!
FROM: Nospmot

Dear Miss Pouty Head:
You chicks are all alike. You think if you give me the silent treatment, I'll buy you a new sweater. Well, no way Hozay. You can stop emailing me all you want because I'm not emailing you either!

Nospmot

TO: Nospmot
FROM: Brittany!!!

Kevin,
No more "Kevvy" for you, Mister! You KNOW I don't wear teddies! They're too hot under my uniform! Wait....you better not be thinking of someone else!!! Maybe you got her confused with me and me with her and that's why you couldn't remember how I got those grass stains. Ooooooooh! It's all starting to make sense now.... That's what you meant by "you chicks are all alike." We're all the same to you, aren't we?

Well, you can stop emailing me because it's over!! And send me back my pictures!!!

Brittany

TO: Brittany!!!
FROM: Nospmot

Dear Brittany,
Huh? What pictures?

Ee Enriched Academics Application, Jodie's

RapidTransmit from DariaM

Nobody likes a flatterer. Oh, wait, sorry. Everybody likes a flatterer.

Send Print

Why do you want to spend this summer at Stanton College's Summer High School Gifted and Talented Program?

~~Rather than relax and enjoy the sun like a normal kid whose father DOESN'T~~
~~think he's raising the next Barbara Jordan,~~ I'm looking forward to taking
advantage of the summer months to further my education at a college with a
rigorous academic program, a distinguished faculty and a diverse student
body ~~but I thought I'd apply to Stanton anyway~~. Stanton is renowned for ~~hav-~~
~~ing been a decent school, oh, 200 years ago~~ educating three signers of the
Declaration of Independence, and it continues to attract the best and the
brightest this nation has to offer ~~if you don't count all the students who go~~
~~to better schools~~. It is for these reasons ~~I just pray I get into one of my first~~
~~choices~~ I hope to spend my summer at Stanton.

Your college also has all the amenities I could ask for: first-rate ~~bus service~~
~~to get the hell off campus~~ resources, proximity to a cultural metropolis for
~~getting the hell off campus~~ cultural activities, and the chance to interact
with professors who are experts in their fields ~~by asking them for a ride off~~
~~campus~~. No wonder Stanton gets thousands of applications from ~~slackers~~ schol-
ars all over the country.

I've pored over your course catalog, and I think the biggest problem I will
have, should I be accepted, is ~~in finding classes that I didn't already take in~~
~~sixth grade~~ deciding which classes to take - there are so many that look inter-
esting. I would also hope to take advantage of the many extracurricular
activities and internship programs you offer, ~~particularly the ones that will~~
~~allow me to get the hell off campus~~.

Thank you for the opportunity to apply to Stanton's Summer High School Gifted
and Talented Program. I hope that, if accepted, my work will bring distinction
to the school ~~or at least some letters of recommendation for college so I can~~
~~get my father off my back. God, I love being a role model~~.

Sincerely,

Retype, then burn this draft

Jodie Landon

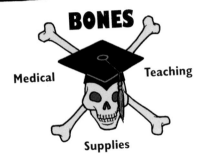

BONES
Medical Teaching Supplies

Box 44533 Asheville, North Carolina 28801
1-800-555-6455

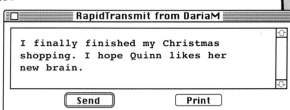

RapidTransmit from DariaM

```
I finally finished my Christmas
shopping. I hope Quinn likes her
new brain.
```

Send   Print

September 6, 1998

Daria Morgendorffer
1111 Glen Oaks Lane
Lawndale

Dear Valued Customer,

According to our records, we have not heard from you in some time. Your business is important to us, so we would like to welcome you back with our preferred customers' discount on our new line of medical teaching supplies. Among the highlights in the winter "Anatomical Abnormalities" catalog:

* Replica of lobotomized brain with visible surgical incisions. Severed nerve fibers with self-adhesive can be reattached to frontal lobes. (Remove before placing in dishwasher.)

* Plaster replica of Belinda and Melinda, Siamese twins joined by their pancreas (38 in. high). Available in white and flesh-tone.

* Cirrhotic liver model covered with fiberlike tissue; liver "opens," showing tissue broken down into fat. Order now and get a second one free for that relative "who can stop anytime."

* Skull model of Phineas Gage, who miraculously survived a railroad accident in which an iron rod was driven through his skull, destroying his moral center. Attention clergy: Perfect for "Hellfire and Brimstone" sermons! Removable rod for easy storage.

* Thoracic Park! Heart-transplant simulator on CD-ROM.

If you have any questions, please don't hesitate to call our toll-free number.
We appreciate your continued patronage.

Sincerely,

"BONES"

T. G. "Bones" Boniske, M.D.
President
Bones Medical Teaching Supplies

P.S. INQUIRE ABOUT OUR FORMALDEHYDE 2000 SERIES OF PRESERVED ANIMALS!

Ff Family Portraits

RapidTransmit from DariaM

A picture says a thousand words, none worth hearing.

Send Print

The Taylors

Cat, *tabby.*
Cats disappear with Brian around, so family no longer bothers coming up with original names like Whiskers.

Brian, 10.
Loves electrical cords, duct tape and the whimper of a helpless animal on a hot afternoon.

Steve, 46, *ad exec.*
Good schmoozer. Would have gone into politics if he had the brains.

Ashley-Amber, 26, *former beer model.*
Met Steve on photo shoot. Laughs at his stale jokes while secretly learning the joint-property laws.

Brittany, 16, *cheerleader, student, living pudding.*
Likes Kevin, books without chapters and Rollerblading with fun new stepmother.
Uses Ashley-Amber's I.D. to get into clubs.

Vivian, 44, *actress/model/ restaurant hostess/ former Mrs. Taylor:*
Shortly after Brian's birth, deserted family to move to Hollywood where people are relatively sane.

The Thompsons

Doug, 35, *contractor.*
Captain of the football team in high school. Could have played in college if he hadn't failed his senior year and a checkpoint test.

Kevin, 17, *football player, student, sieve.*
Believes Mom and Dad when they tell him he's the handsomest, smartest, wittiest man alive.
Taught Dad how to make underarm noises.

Charlene, 35, *housewife.*
Loves to see her reflection in the shine of Kevin's freshly polished trophy. Doesn't think that tramp Brittany is good enough for her son.

The Griffins

Tom, 45, *CPA.*
Still questions whether he should have married plain Patty Wells instead. "She was always so happy to see me and such a good sport. Still, there was that mole…"

Linda, 43, *VP of marketing for KSBC.*
Still harping on her brief career as a news anchor twenty years ago: "Did I ever tell you about my interview with Rosalynn Carter?"

Sandi, 16, *president of the Fashion Club, student.*
Aspiring fashion commentator.
Hopes Quinn will get that disease that causes all your hair to fall out.

Sam, 12, *student, brat.*
Never outgrew the "terrible twos." Likes to pound his brother, kick walls and fill the house with water.
Plans someday to marry Quinn.

Chris, 10, *student, brat.*
Likes to pound his brother back, pick at scabs (anyone's) and watch things drop.
Plans someday to marry Quinn.

The Landons

Andrew, 50, *entrepreneur.*
Nouveau riche and proud of it. Loves his baby boy even more than his new Jag. Hates welfare cheats, taxes and unimaginative accountants.

Jodie, 16, *superstudent.*
Could possibly become this country's first African-American and female president if the stress of being perfect doesn't kill her first.

Rachel, 11, *so-so student.*
"I hate you, you little monster. I was the baby of the family, but nooooo, you had to come along and ruin everything…"

Michele, 42, *former VP, now full-time mother.*
Had to quit her high-powered job when their unplanned son was born–but it's *okay*. Nurses to *Wall Street World*.

Evan, 6 months, *baby:*
"Help."

Ff Fave Folks from History, Daria's

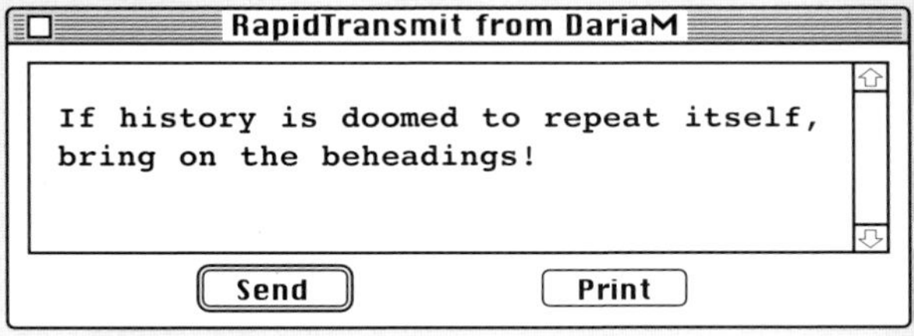
RapidTransmit from DariaM
If history is doomed to repeat itself, bring on the beheadings!
Send
Print

John Calvin (1509-64)
Promoted predestination: the idea that God has already decided who will be saved and who will go to hell, and there's nothing you can do about it, so why even get out of bed?

Cleopatra VII (69–30 B.C.)
Early tabloid queen. Married her brother, shacked up with Caesar, killed off her brother, and married Marc Antony. Mercifully ended it all before she became a burden to her children.

Huangdi, Shi of the Qin Dynasty (reigned 221–206 B.C.)
Admirable fear of strangers and the world. The first to unify the Chinese Empire, misanthropic Shi started the Great Wall. Inspiration for the project I'm building in my room.

Guevara, Che (1928–67)
Gave up what could have been a thriving medical practice performing unnecessary operations for a career in guerrilla warfare. So what if he never bathed?

Guillotin, Joseph (1738–1814)
Found a quick and sanitary way to execute the masses and stop all that whining during the Reign of Terror. Timesaving guillotine took the guesswork out of beheadings and eliminated painful "executioner blister."

van Gogh, Vincent (1853-90)
Postimpressionist paintings gave dementia a good name. So he cut off his ear, fought with Gauguin, hung out in insane asylums and committed suicide. Nobody's perfect.

Ff Food in Film

RapidTransmit from DariaM

I wish people spoke in subtitles.
Then I could just close my eyes.

Send Print

PLAYHOUSE 99
Food in Film Festival

FOOD IN FILM:

A Celebration of Gustatory Cinema

"THE PIE"

"The Pie" (Part I) (Italian 1965): Leave it to Italian cinema to turn something as wholesome as blueberry pie into a campy aphrodisiac. Surprisingly poignant; when Sophia smothers herself in blueberry-pie filling, is she not hiding herself, physically and emotionally, from Donatello, her ardent and much younger lover? Pie-throwing scene ruins what could have been a very tender finale.

"FRANCOIS the SEEDLESS"

"Francois the Seedless" (French 1959): Vintner Francois's obsession with seedless (and therefore impotent) grapes symbolizes his inability to choose between enlisting in the French Army or remaining true to his Algerian homeland. The sequence featuring the discovery of a rat's head in a Bordeaux bottle led to improved sanitary controls throughout the nation's wineries.

"THE PIE" II

"The Pie" (Part II) (Italian 1996): In this sequel made thirty years later, Donatello looks up his old love, Sophia, in a small Italian village. This time it's Donatello who's hiding behind the sugar and glaze, ashamed of his shiftless life. True love never dies, however, and the blueberry filling is every bit as appetizing as it was thirty years before. Damn pie-throwing wrecks what should have been a sensual reunion.

"O YEAST!"

"O Yeast!" (Irish 1979): Based on the true story of suicidal poet Margaret O'Sullivan, "O Yeast!" chronicles the poet's formative childhood years spent confined in the flour bin of her father's bakery. The underlying message is that the human spirit, like yeast, is ever expanding, until baked to a crisp.

"CORIANDER MY LOVE"

"Coriander My Love" (Chinese 1979): Amid the torrid backdrop of the Cultural Revolution, this timeless love story looks at Mao Ze-dong's epic romance with starlet Chiang Ch'ing. The infamous "wok scene," in which Chiang brutally minces the coriander, is not for the fainthearted.

"YAM, MA'AM"

"Yam, Ma'am" (American 1968): Set in Kissimmee, Florida, this German-financed musical romp follows the plight of the luckless DuWitts, yam farmers who lose their entire crop to a sinkhole. Crisis hot lines were flooded with calls after audiences saw little Jimbo dive after the yams and lose his life.

"ANDRE SAKARINSKI'S LAST MEAL"

"Andre Sakarinski's Last Meal" (USSR 1938): Blini and borscht stand in for the bourgeoisie and the proletariat in this post-Revolution satire. Are social classes the same once they've been digested? The execution scene is said to have inspired the denouement of "House Party II."

lay House 99
Downtown
awndale

Gothic Nights The Adventures of Queen Hecuba

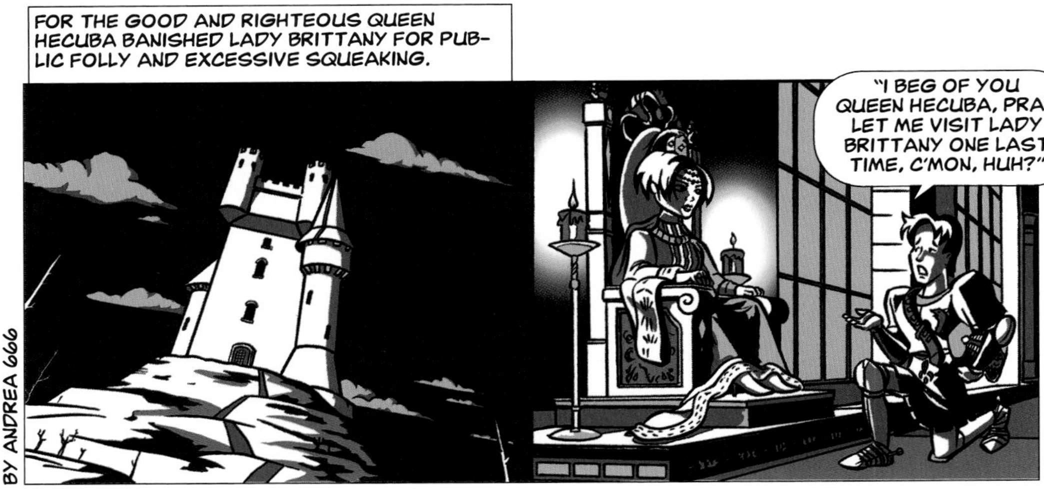
FOR THE GOOD AND RIGHTEOUS QUEEN HECUBA BANISHED LADY BRITTANY FOR PUBLIC FOLLY AND EXCESSIVE SQUEAKING.
"I BEG OF YOU QUEEN HECUBA, PRAY LET ME VISIT LADY BRITTANY ONE LAST TIME, C'MON, HUH?"
BY ANDREA 666

AND SO IT WAS THAT QUEEN HECUBA RAISED CHARLES'S RANK FROM COURT JESTER TO DUKE.
"NOW I CANNETH NOT MISS WITH THE LADIES!"
"YOUR FIRST DUTY IS TO SECURE THE RELEASE OF MY BELOVED BROTHER, DAMIEN, FROM EVIL KING JOHN."
BY ANDREA 666

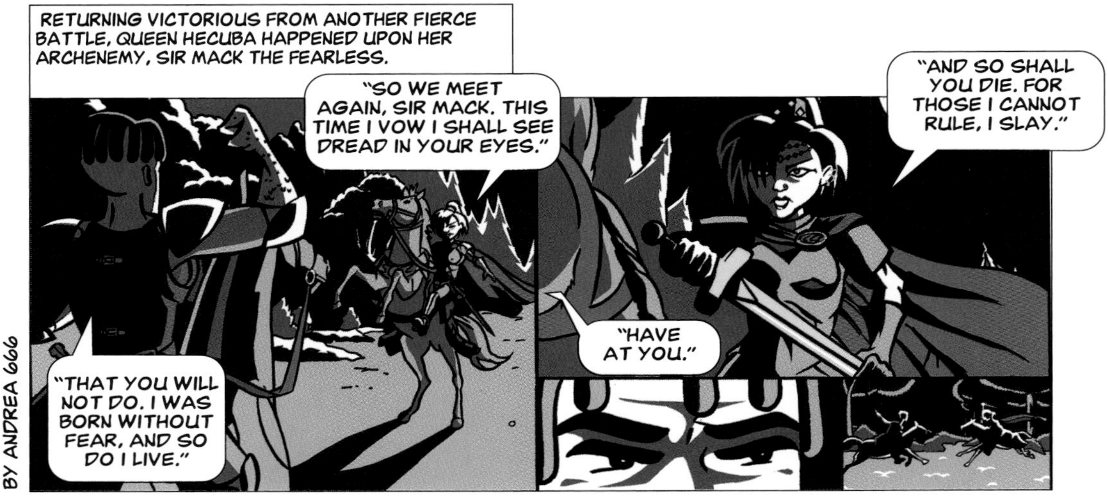
RETURNING VICTORIOUS FROM ANOTHER FIERCE BATTLE, QUEEN HECUBA HAPPENED UPON HER ARCHENEMY, SIR MACK THE FEARLESS.
"SO WE MEET AGAIN, SIR MACK. THIS TIME I VOW I SHALL SEE DREAD IN YOUR EYES."
"THAT YOU WILL NOT DO. I WAS BORN WITHOUT FEAR, AND SO DO I LIVE."
"AND SO SHALL YOU DIE. FOR THOSE I CANNOT RULE, I SLAY."
"HAVE AT YOU."
BY ANDREA 666

RapidTransmit from DariaM
Personally, I think the scariest thing about the Middle Ages was the hygiene.
Send
Print
SO QUEEN HECUBA KINDLY GRANTED KNIGHT KEVIN HIS WISH.
"KEVVY!"
"HEY!"
"BRILLIANT USING LADY BRITTANY AS BAIT."
"THAT'S THE LAST TIME SIR KEVIN SINGS CHUMBAWUMBA ON THE BATTLEFIELD. IDIOT."
"GRRRRRR!"
Trade you this duke for my brother?
"BUT I'M ONLY A COURT JESTER! I SWEARETH!"
"PREVARICATOR. YOU'RE NOT EVEN FUNNY."
"WAIT! I JUST REMEMBERED... I LEFT THE TOASTER OVEN ON!"
"HELLO, DEAR. YOUR FRIEND WAS IN QUITE A HURRY."
"HAVE YOU ANY INTEREST IN A GOVERNMENT JOB?"

Gg Greetings from Brookside Rest Home

BROOKSIDE
REST HOME

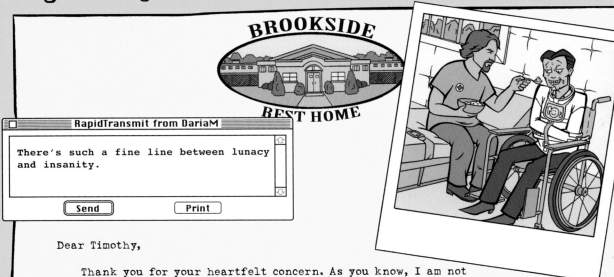

RapidTransmit from DariaM

There's such a fine line between lunacy and insanity.

Send Print

Dear Timothy,

Thank you for your heartfelt concern. As you know, I am not an angry man and do not know myself why I reacted in the way I did. Perhaps it was the stress of wasting twenty years of my life trying to teach the unteachable, unable to convey to these dissipated scions of affluence basic fundamentals easily grasped by any chimpanzee possessing a passing familiarity with sign language. Or maybe I was just having a bad day. It is a relief that Kevin and his family have decided not to pursue the matter any further, though, between us, I doubt whether their lawsuit alleging "psychological trauma" would have progressed very far, dependent as it was on the boy demonstrating any PSYCHOLOGY at all. Hold on, I think perhaps I should take some MEDICATION.

Better. Although I initially resisted coming here, I have to confess that I'm feeling much more relaxed and clearheaded than I have in years, even though they tell me it has only been two weeks since I entered this establishment. I do not profess to be an expert on institutional decor, but I believe there is something very soothing about the faded yellow paint, for I have never slepp so well in my lif.

I hope zat temprarly assuming my teaching responsbilities hazzn placed an untold burden on zoo. I's zure in good time I'll be back to hearz the shatter of stussens as ze discuzzas figers of greaz imporzance like tellvijun slars an makpp tpssssss

KILL ALL THE BRUTES

From the desk of
TIMOTHY O'NEILL

Dear Anthony,
Don't worry about your classes. All is going well!
You just concentrate on getting better!
T. O'N.

RapidTransmit from DariaM

I tried to get Quinn to play "Shallow Grave," but she was afraid the dirt would mess up her hair.

Send Print

GUESS THE FAMOUS MENTAL CASE

This is an ideal game to play with the whole family. The object is for player one to pick someone famous and act out his or her psychiatric symptoms. The other players have to guess the person you're thinking of, along with the medical condition. If they don't guess the correct answer within one minute, player one gets to act out someone new. The game is over when one player manages to stump the others three times. Ready? I'll start:

Playtime over. I'm going to my room now.

(Answers: 1. Winston Churchill, depression; 2. Martin Luther, depression; 3. Leo Tolstoy, depression.)

Hh Handout, Teen Anxiety, How to Reduce

HOW TO REDUCE TEEN ANXIETY

Courtesy of
LAWNDALE DERMATOLOGICAL ASSOCIATES
773 GROVE STREET

Being a teen is not easy. As we leave childhood behind, we undergo all kinds of physical and emotional changes that are wonderful, miraculous—and, yes, confusing. Add to that the daily pressure of the perilous P's—passing tests, popularity and pimples—and it's no wonder that one day anxiety may suddenly appear on our doorstep like an exchange student who has renounced his citizenship and come to stay for good! But just as hosting an exchange student provides us with an opportunity for wonderful learning experiences, there's a bright side to becoming riddled with anxiety, probably. Perhaps not, but anyway, worrying too much is bad for your skin. The teen years don't have to be fraught with anguish. Here are a few tried-and-true suggestions to get you through these tumultuous times:

FROM MOM
FROM DAD

Look on the bright side
Even the most dire situation has a silver lining. Let's say you failed a class, have to take summer school and won't be able to go with your friends on that trip to Europe you've been planning for six months. That's just an opportunity to make *new* friends—ones who don't need to go all the way to another continent to find their "kicks"! Or suppose your boyfriend breaks up with you the night before the senior prom because he wants to take someone else. Now's your chance to "play the field," or maybe even experiment with an alternative lifestyle that doesn't involve boys at all! Or perhaps you're being expelled from school altogether because of your repeated assaults on other students, and your parents are splitting up because they can no longer cope with the strain caused by your behavior. Let the gift parade begin as they try to outbid each other for your affections! See? Find that silver lining and focus on it!

Parents are your friends, too
If something's bothering you, don't hesitate to share with Mom and Dad. They're on *your* side. Say you don't have anyone to "hang out" with on Saturday. Maybe you and Mom can go to the mall and try on clothes together. School bully picking on you? Ask Dad to have a talk with him! If you're not invited to a party maybe your parents can call the parents of the girl who's having the party and insist that you be put on "the list." Remember, parents were teenagers once. They know your pain and can help you through it.

RapidTransmit from DariaM

I've been suspicious of doctors ever since one showed up at my birth. I didn't invite him.

Send   Print

<u>Visit your school counselor</u>

Your school counselor is a special person—someone who cares so much about young people and their problems that he or she has devoted his or her life to helping them. In fact, school counselors often forsake higher-paying jobs in the private sector to remain on their watch, necessitating a string of demeaning freelance jobs to make ends meet and culminating in the so-called writing of a series of insipid "advice" pamphlets underwritten by the manufacturers of useless acne remedies and left to gather dust in the waiting rooms of cow-town dermatologists' offices. I bet no one at Scutter Pharmaceuticals ever even reads this far, and if they do, I don't care. Cheap, moronic bastards. So seek out your school counselor, and give a good listen to what he or she has to tell you. In times of trouble, there's no substitute for the friendly advice of a trained, objective observer.

DONT BE SAD... ...GET GLAD!

<u>Get over it</u>

Believe it or not, someday when you can't meet the mortgage, or develop a gravely serious disease, you'll be kicking yourself for the way you worried about your petty teenage problems. Remember: No one ever needed an organ transplant because they were voted "most unpopular"! Remember, too, that many famous people weren't well-liked or even very attractive. Take Albert Einstein. He was never voted "best body," and he turned out okay. Similarly, history tells us that Hitler was virtually ignored by the popular group at his high school, although that's probably a bad example. But you get the idea: Cheer up! And send Anxiety packing back to the impoverished little nation it came from!

DARIA,
This will help you control
that RASH!
OR maybe not.
DR. D

Ii Interesting Paintings, Jane's

ONE OF THE MORE UPLIFTING ART MOVEMENTS, CUBISM POINTS OUT THE LIGHTER SIDE OF DISLOCATION AND DISMEMBERMENT.

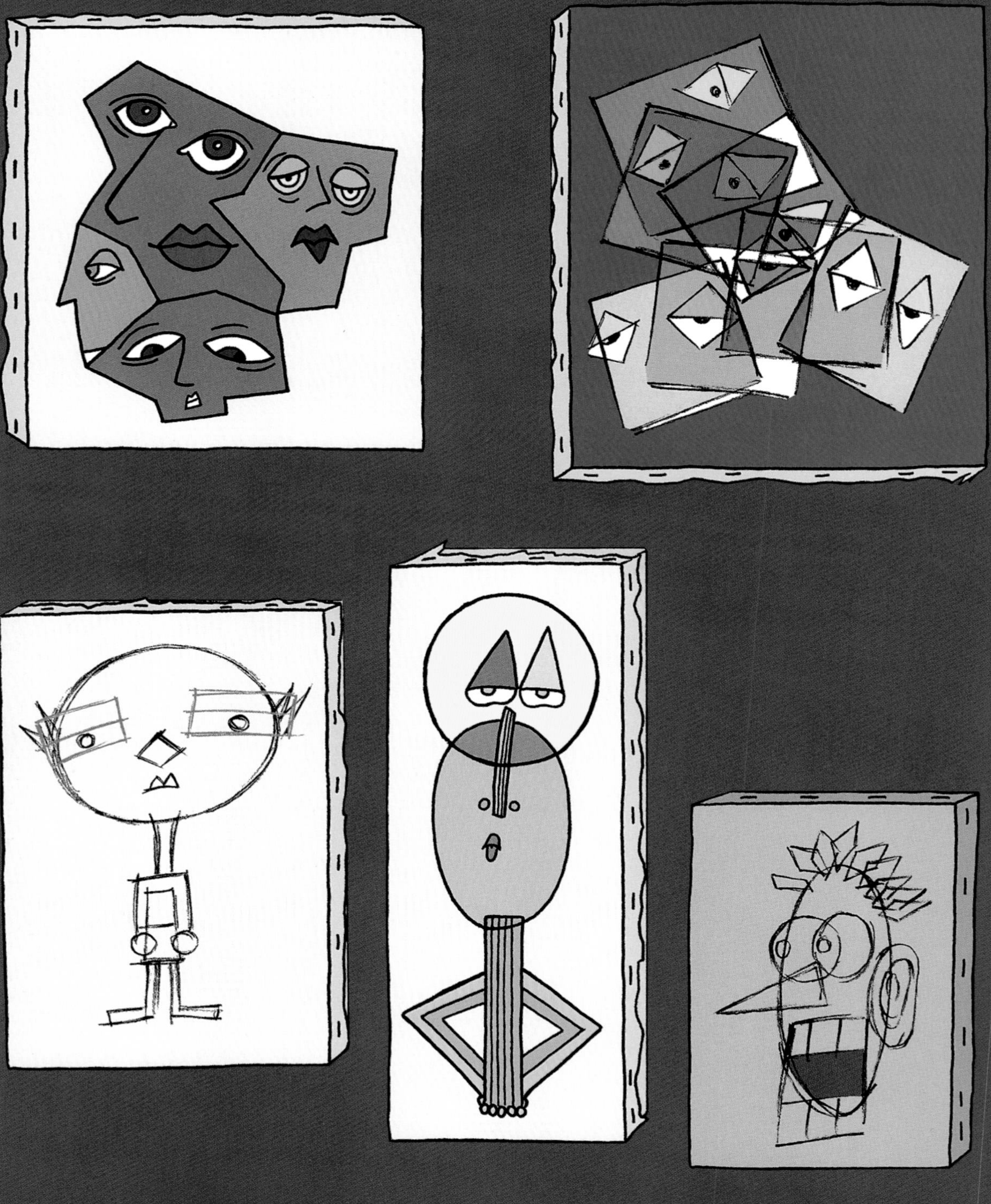

MYSTIK SPIRAL

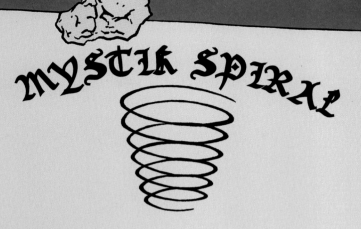

Yo, whassup Spiralmaniacs! Word from me, Danny M, recording secretary of the Mystik Spiral Fan Club. You're like, "What's with this mailing? The next newsletter isn't due 'til summer!" True enough, but this is a Special Edition. Trent, Max, Nick, and my big brother Jesse (who's asked me to teach him diminished chords) have passed along some excellent news from Spiral Central—the band tells me that plans for their Spring Tour of Carter County are tentatively firm. I stayed up for three days straight making this map, but check it out—time well spent if you ask me! I even put in, like, travelers' conveniences and points of interest and whatnot.

In other Spiral news, I've been practicing day and night (except when I take time off for stuff like the newsletter and this map)—just between you and me, by this time next year I bet I'm a full-fledged member of the Spiral! (I'm pretty sure two of the guys would already vote to let me join, so I just need, like, one more on my side.) And I've got a LOT of song ideas—so when I do join the Spiral, I guarantee you'll hear a difference! Anyway, see ya at the Spiral Spring Tour!

Peace,

Danny

RapidTransmit from DariaM

Well, I hear they're very big in Japan.

Send | Print

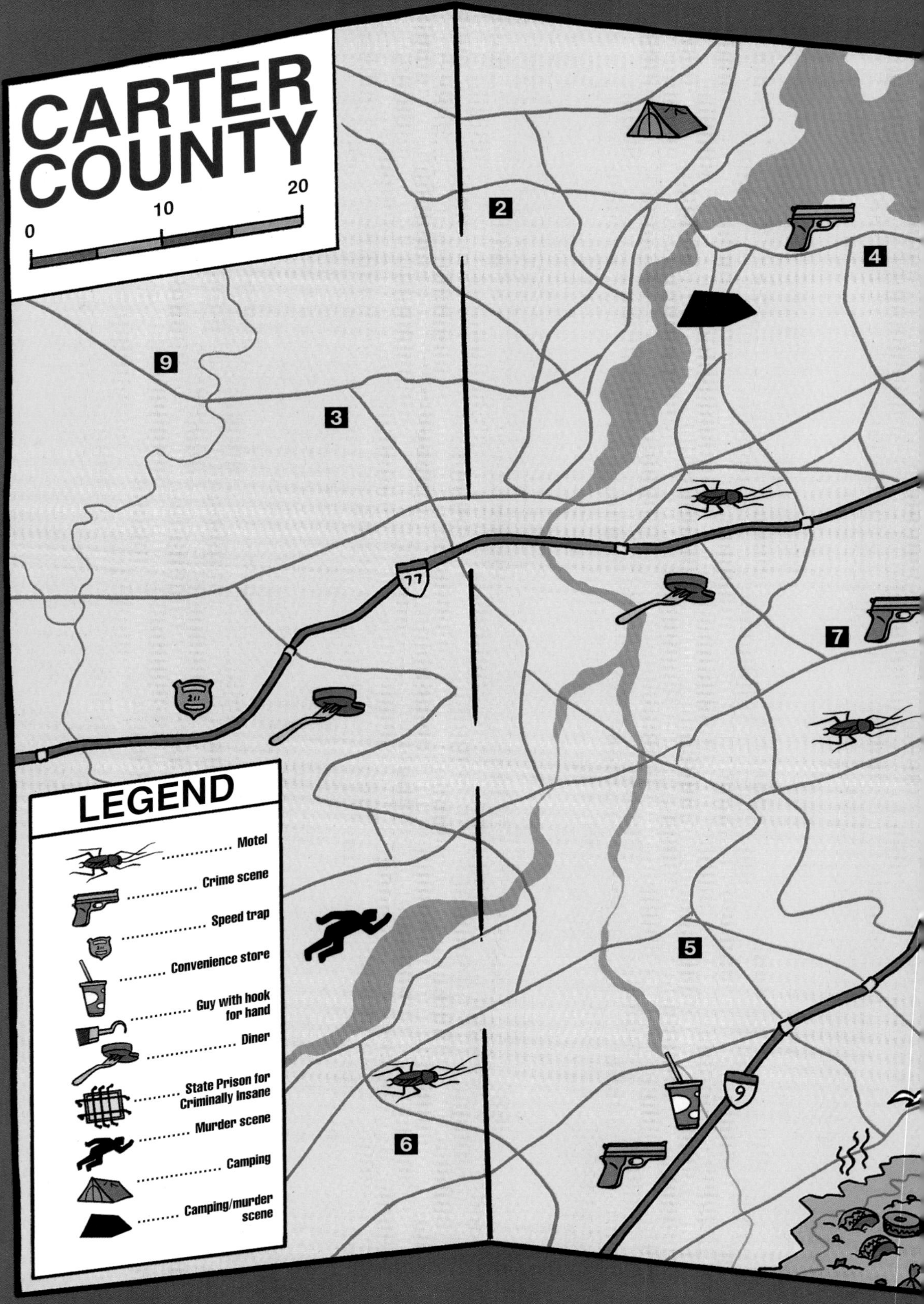
CARTER COUNTY
0
10
20
2
4
9
3
77
7
5
9
6
LEGEND
Motel
Crime scene
Speed trap
Convenience store
Guy with hook for hand
Diner
State Prison for Criminally Insane
Murder scene
Camping
Camping/murder scene

8
77
10
9
11

List of clubs:

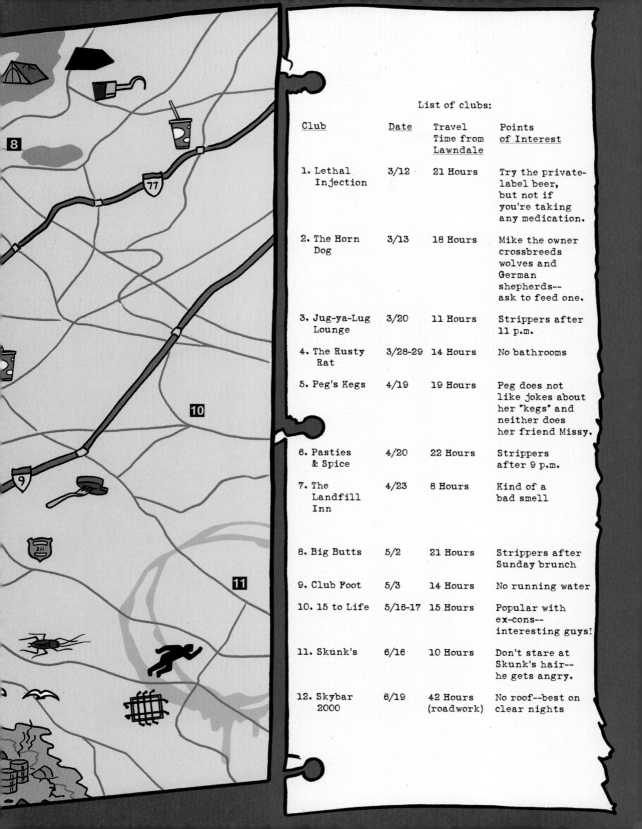

Club	Date	Travel Time from Lawndale	Points of Interest
1. Lethal Injection	3/12	21 Hours	Try the private-label beer, but not if you're taking any medication.
2. The Horn Dog	3/13	18 Hours	Mike the owner crossbreeds wolves and German shepherds--ask to feed one.
3. Jug-ya-Lug Lounge	3/20	11 Hours	Strippers after 11 p.m.
4. The Rusty Rat	3/28-29	14 Hours	No bathrooms
5. Peg's Kegs	4/19	19 Hours	Peg does not like jokes about her "kegs" and neither does her friend Missy.
6. Pasties & Spice	4/20	22 Hours	Strippers after 9 p.m.
7. The Landfill Inn	4/23	8 Hours	Kind of a bad smell
8. Big Butts	5/2	21 Hours	Strippers after Sunday brunch
9. Club Foot	5/3	14 Hours	No running water
10. 15 to Life	5/16-17	15 Hours	Popular with ex-cons--interesting guys!
11. Skunk's	6/16	10 Hours	Don't stare at Skunk's hair--he gets angry.
12. Skybar 2000	6/19	42 Hours (roadwork)	No roof--best on clear nights

JIM'S PAINTBALLING JUNGLE

Miss those glory days in 'Nam, Grenada, Kuwait—or, worse, never seen combat duty at all? Worried this namby-pamby world is gonna turn your kid into a sissy? Want to see if the guy you're dating is a real man? Then come on down to Jim's Paintballing Jungle and visit one of our five gut-wrenching fields for some good old-fashioned family fun! Look what $60 gets you:

UN

URBAN TOWN

RENTAL GUN, AMMO, AMMO AND MORE AMMO!

JIMBALL 1000 Full/Semiautomatic with customized sniper barrel, 300 shots per ounce CO_2. Rapid-firing velocity will make you yearn for a real war—or maybe start one!

Granite-Master Paintballs–Banned in 49 states, these superaccurate, superfast spheres of sheer beauty will give your weenie challengers welts to write home about.

Gore's Grenade 4000. I said it in 'Nam, and I'll say it here: Bull's-eye is bull*!$#! Good aim is *not* a necessity when you lob one of these babies! Limit one per customer. (Tear gas extra.)

RapidTransmit from DariaM

Bring the family and take a break from all that violence on TV.

Send   Print

JIM'S PAINTBALLING CALENDAR

Not sold in stores, each month of this gun-lover's calendar features a different firearm in all her cold, blue finery. Important dates—Samuel Colt's death, the debut of the AK-47, the birth of Charlton Heston—are also duly noted.

ACCESS TO FIVE EXPLOSIVE PLAYING FIELDS, INCLUDING:

Iraq
Once the Garden of Eden, Baghdad is now the handbasket to hell. Labyrinths of underground bunkers and tunnels are exact replicas of where chicken-man Saddam hides whenever our valiant boys make his army eat sand!

Bosnia
Serbs, Croats, Muslims, who cares? Get 'em all! It's a battlefield out there, chock-full of rolling hills and dense brush for fun sniper action. Downed crybaby U.N. helicopter perfect for picnics.

AUGUST

S	M	T	W	T	F	S
						1
2	3	4	5	6	7	8
9	10	11	12	13	14	15
16	17	18	19	20	21	22
23/30	24/31	25	26	27	28	29

Urbantown, U.S.A.
Our cities have deteriorated into aboveground sewers where vermin and filth prey on the meek from the comfort of abandoned buildings and tenement slums. Prowl the cracked sidewalks and sniper-riddled rooftops, and you'll swear you're home!

Hours: We're open from 9 a.m. to 6 p.m., seven days a week; Christmas and holidays, 9 a.m. to midnight.

Available for weddings, bachelor parties, and group counseling sessions. 50% discount for vets, bounty hunters and mercenaries.

Disclaimer

Jim's Paintballing Jungle is not responsible for any welts, bruises, or loss of eyes. We make every effort to maintain bridges, barracks, tunnels, shooting decks, interrogation rooms, bamboo cages, electrical cords, shackles, shallow graves, solitary confinement boxes and other structures, but are not responsible, should collapse or accident occur, for broken backs, limbs, bones, spinal injuries, paralysis, death, or Post-Paintball Traumatic Stress Syndrome.

Jj Journalistic Photo Essay

Socially concerned high school students debate the issues that will determine their futures. Today's topics: scrunchy colors and how to make butter stick to ceilings.

Student statement re: the issue of First Amendment rights versus the right to privacy as it applies to Monday mornings.

From the desk of
TIMOTHY O'NEILL

PHOTOGRAPHIC ESSAY: MR. O'NEILL
Due 1/23
Dear Class: Words are one way to tell a story. Pictures are another. Put them together, and you get narrative dynamite! Make a "big bang" with a photographic essay illustrating the pressures, pleasures, and uncertainties of high school today.

RapidTransmit from DariaM

The trick to photojournalism is to make people forget you're there. I'm good at that.

Send | Print

Semantics class.
Deconstructing "postfeminist" until it means "kissable."

LAWNDALE HIGH SCHOOL
EXIT

...ific
...on.

Philosophy.
"But what if Hegel was right?"

Satisfying the unquenchable thirst for knowledge.

"Is that a yes or a no?"

Another triumphant day of learning comes to a close. Twenty-first century, here we come!

Kk Keeping Your Piercing Clean

Axl's
PIERCING PARLOR

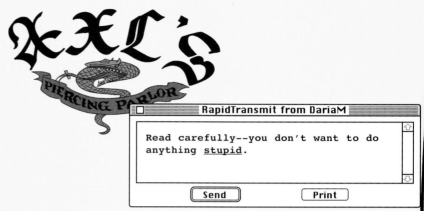

RapidTransmit from DariaM

Read carefully--you don't want to do anything <u>stupid</u>.

Send | Print

KEEP YOUR BLOODY TONGUE CLEAN

Cheers and congratulations on your new tongue barbell and thank you for choosing Axl's Piercing Parlor for your body adornment needs. Because Axl's employs a groundbreaking dual-sterilization method (each needle is held over the stove *and* a match, and I'm talking about those big wooden ones), you are assured a better-than-even chance of suffering no permanent side effects. But in case something does come up, here are a few simple instructions that we in no way recommend as a substitute for immediate professional medical attention:

Swelling: Swelling will probably go down in a week or whenever, but you can minimize any soreness by sucking on ice or biting a bullet. While post-pierce eating is occasionally still physically possible, it is not recommended for the first fourteen days following your procedure. Some customers have reported managing to survive this period by subsisting on an all-applesauce diet, but Axl's does *not* advise this, because applesauce contains enzymes that can really dull the shine of your barbell.

Mucusy yellow stuff: Relax! It's a sign that your tongue is healing, so the oozier the better. As a common courtesy, however, avoid getting your tongue too close to friends, no matter how this may impact your normal lifestyle.

Keep the tongue clean: Regular cleaning is important, so be sure to brush your teeth several times a week. Rinsing with an antiseptic mouthwash is okay, but *don't swallow*. And don't forget the piercing rim. Use a cotton swab to remove any crusting, scabs, metallic flakes, fleshy bits or unidentifiable objects from the disfigured area of your tongue. (See above mouthwash instructions re: swallowing this material.) And please: Don't share swabs.

Do not remove your barbell until all symptoms are finito. Taking out your barbell can cause piercing close-up and then we'll have to punch a hole in your bloody tongue all over again. And there's no discount for a heal job, mate, so don't even ask me.

Beer/wines/spirits: nature's disinfectants. Alcohol is an excellent sterilizer and has superb numbing qualities (just ask any sot who's been beat up). Unlike mouthwash, you needn't worry about inadvertently swallowing it—in fact, many of our clients report that spirits decrease their appetite for painful solid meals.

Remember, Axl's stands behind its work. If for any reason you have more serious complications than those listed above, feel free to call us *immediately,* although your insurance won't cover our treatment, so you'd be much, much better off going to a doctor and not mentioning Axl's at all. Say you fell on a pen or something.

Axl

Not responsible for any swelling, tearing, ripping, shredding, discoloration, discomfort, disability, disorientation, infections, infarctions, infractions, yellowy mucusy stuff, or amputation.
Thank you for choosing Axl's!

Kk Kevin's Party Trick

RapidTransm
Curiously, only Ke
potential as a dec
Send

How to remove a cork from a wine bottle by using only a string.

1. Remove bottle from friends' parents' wine cellar. Older bottles are better 'cause the cork's soggier and easier to push through. Get spares in case the first bottle breaks. Oh, yeah, Brittany says don't forget Band-Aids, just in case. Girls! ▶

Chateau du Arriviste
1978

2. Remove metal stuff f
careful not to cut you
then, pushing really
cork into the bottle.
◀ try, depending on st

3. Pour out wine, so bottle is half full. ▶

4. Take a foot-long piece of string (about half a yard) and tie the bottom of the string into a circle. ▶

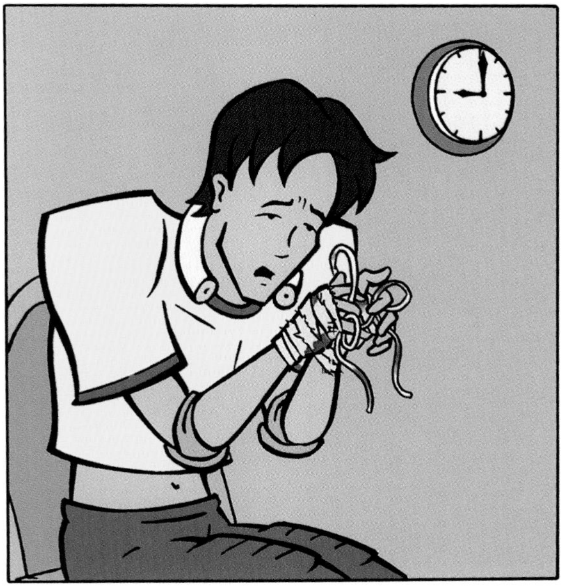

5. Insert the string into bottle and try to fit the circle ◀ over the small end of the cork.

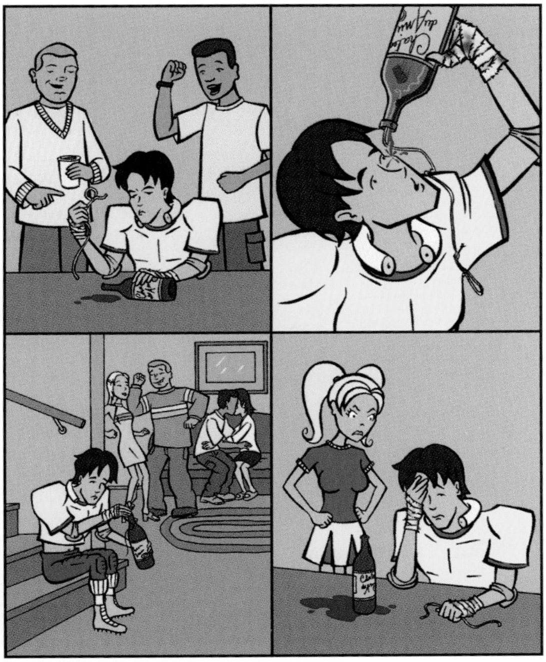

6. I know I know how to do this! ▶

Kk Kinsington Prison, Daria's E-mail to

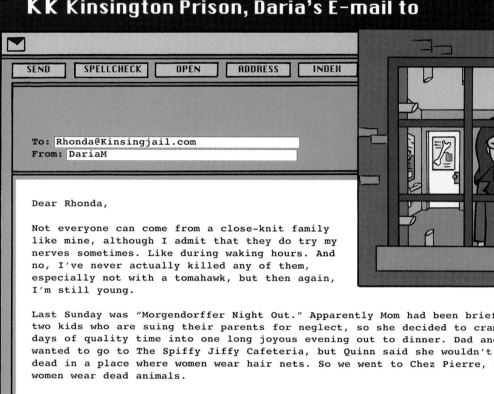

SEND SPELLCHECK OPEN ADDRESS INDEX

To: Rhonda@Kinsingjail.com
From: DariaM

Dear Rhonda,

Not everyone can come from a close-knit family like mine, although I admit that they do try my nerves sometimes. Like during waking hours. And no, I've never actually killed any of them, especially not with a tomahawk, but then again, I'm still young.

Last Sunday was "Morgendorffer Night Out." Apparently Mom had been brief
two kids who are suing their parents for neglect, so she decided to cran
days of quality time into one long joyous evening out to dinner. Dad anc
wanted to go to The Spiffy Jiffy Cafeteria, but Quinn said she wouldn't
dead in a place where women wear hair nets. So we went to Chez Pierre,
women wear dead animals.

We caught up with one another's lives before our drink orders, and then
to take a business call. I gave Dad some sections of my paper, and Quinn
to another table with a guy she'd met in the coat-check line. All in al
successful evening. I can't wait for family bonding night again next yea

There's something I want to ask you. Why do they consider solitary confi
punishment? To me, three meals a day and no one around to bother you wou
damn sight better than parole.

Good luck with your appeal.

Daria

RapidTransmit from

The biggest advantage to
getting out and telling
friends you weren't real
abroad.

Send

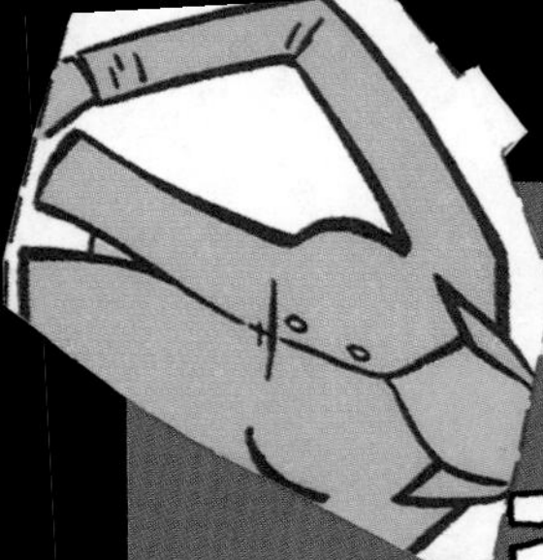

ble Sketches, Jane's

DEPICTING PEOPLE AS THEY REALLY ARE AND NOT HOW THEY SEE THEMSELVES MADE GOYA FAMOUS. IT JUST GIVES ME SOMETHING TO DO DURING MATH.

LI Lawndale High's Teacher's Lounge

1
3
TOILET SEAT COVERS
2

Mr. O'Neill's

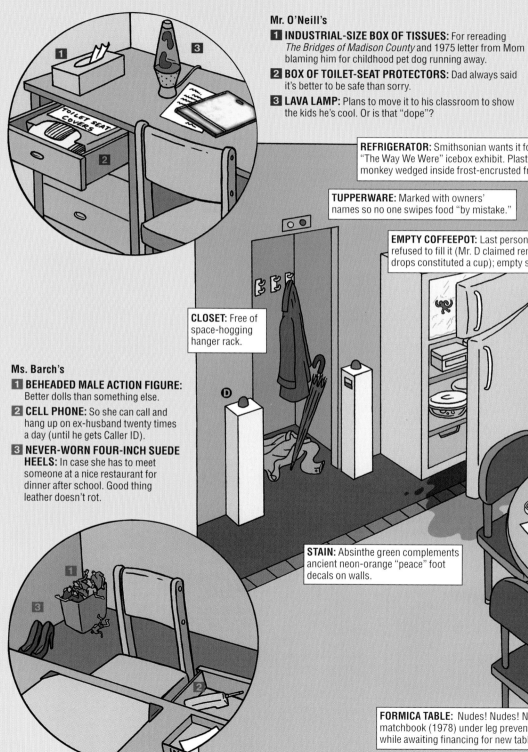

1 INDUSTRIAL-SIZE BOX OF TISSUES: For rereading *The Bridges of Madison County* and 1975 letter from Mom blaming him for childhood pet dog running away.

2 BOX OF TOILET-SEAT PROTECTORS: Dad always said it's better to be safe than sorry.

3 LAVA LAMP: Plans to move it to his classroom to show the kids he's cool. Or is that "dope"?

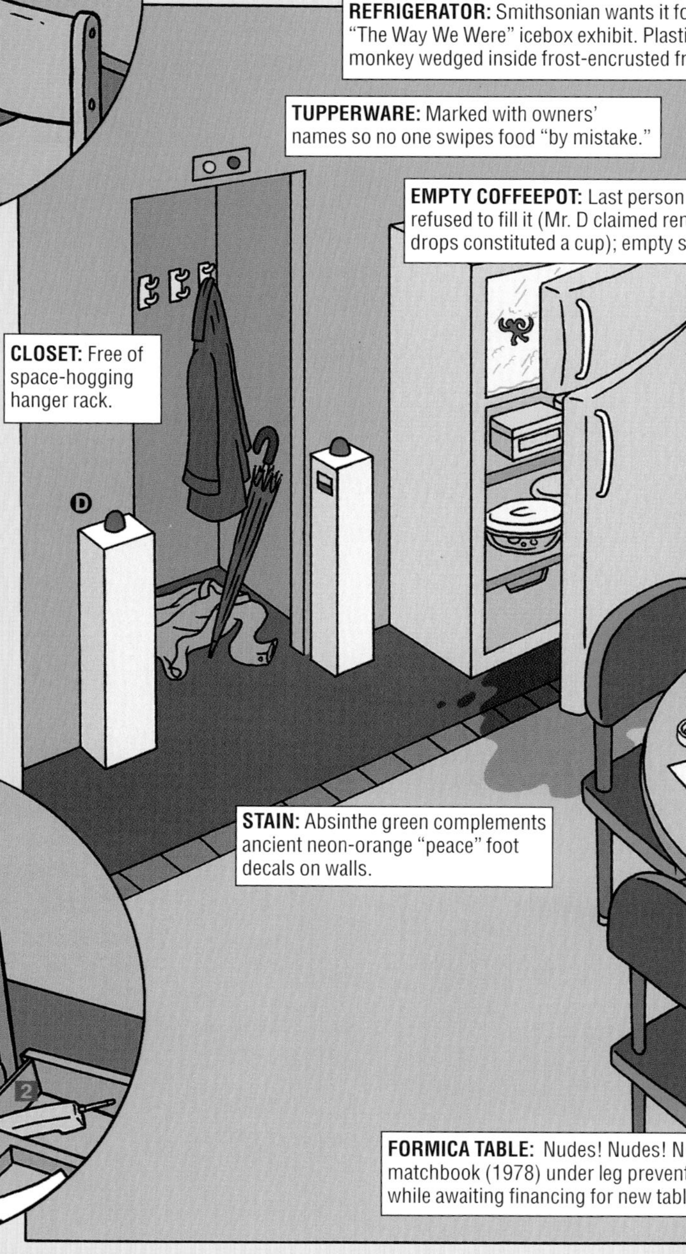
REFRIGERATOR: Smithsonian wants it fo
"The Way We Were" icebox exhibit. Plasti
monkey wedged inside frost-encrusted fr
TUPPERWARE: Marked with owners' names so no one swipes food "by mistake."
EMPTY COFFEEPOT: Last person
refused to fill it (Mr. D claimed rem
drops constituted a cup); empty s
CLOSET: Free of space-hogging hanger rack.
D
STAIN: Absinthe green complements ancient neon-orange "peace" foot decals on walls.
FORMICA TABLE: Nudes! Nudes! N
matchbook (1978) under leg prevent
while awaiting financing for new tabl

Ms. Barch's

1 BEHEADED MALE ACTION FIGURE: Better dolls than something else.

2 CELL PHONE: So she can call and hang up on ex-husband twenty times a day (until he gets Caller ID).

3 NEVER-WORN FOUR-INCH SUEDE HEELS: In case she has to meet someone at a nice restaurant for dinner after school. Good thing leather doesn't rot.

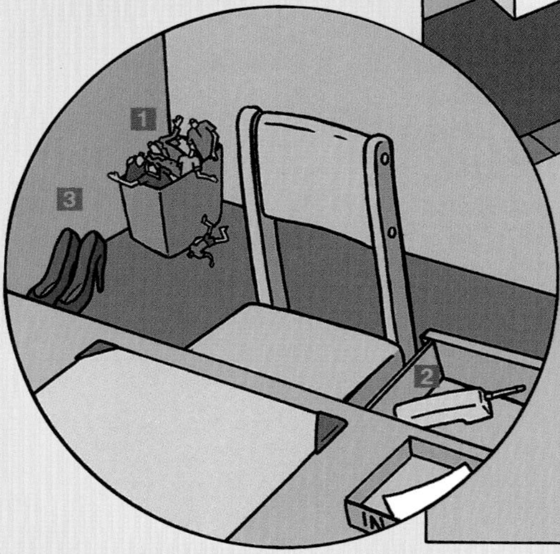
1
3
2
IN

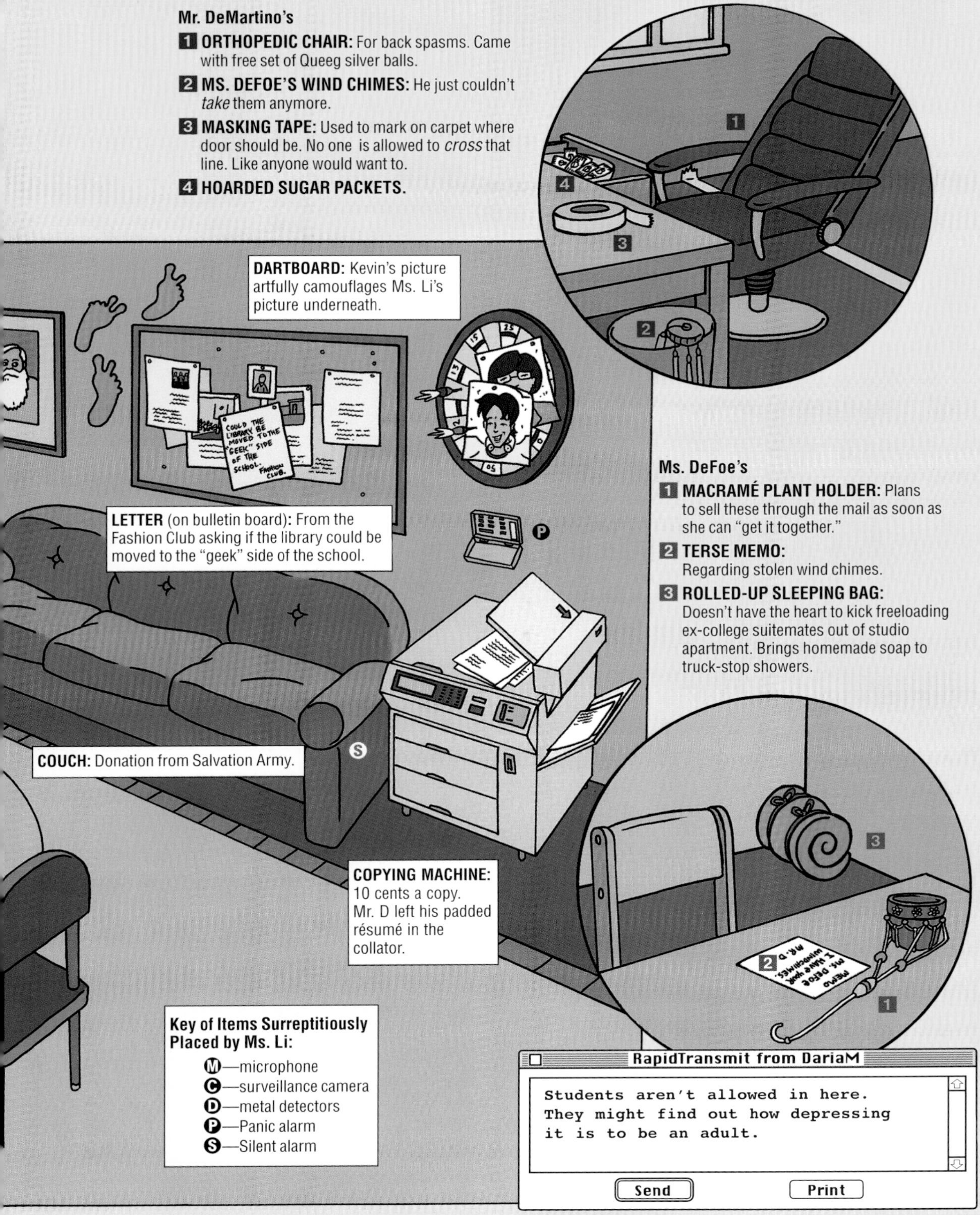

COULD THE LIBRARY BE MOVED TO THE "GEEK" SIDE OF THE SCHOOL. FASHION CLUB.

Mr. DeMartino's

1. **ORTHOPEDIC CHAIR:** For back spasms. Came with free set of Queeg silver balls.
2. **MS. DEFOE'S WIND CHIMES:** He just couldn't *take* them anymore.
3. **MASKING TAPE:** Used to mark on carpet where door should be. No one is allowed to *cross* that line. Like anyone would want to.
4. **HOARDED SUGAR PACKETS.**

DARTBOARD: Kevin's picture artfully camouflages Ms. Li's picture underneath.

LETTER (on bulletin board)**:** From the Fashion Club asking if the library could be moved to the "geek" side of the school.

COUCH: Donation from Salvation Army.

COPYING MACHINE: 10 cents a copy. Mr. D left his padded résumé in the collator.

Ms. DeFoe's

1. **MACRAMÉ PLANT HOLDER:** Plans to sell these through the mail as soon as she can "get it together."
2. **TERSE MEMO:** Regarding stolen wind chimes.
3. **ROLLED-UP SLEEPING BAG:** Doesn't have the heart to kick freeloading ex-college suitemates out of studio apartment. Brings homemade soap to truck-stop showers.

Key of Items Surreptitiously Placed by Ms. Li:

- Ⓜ—microphone
- Ⓒ—surveillance camera
- Ⓓ—metal detectors
- Ⓟ—Panic alarm
- Ⓢ—Silent alarm

RapidTransmit from DariaM

```
Students aren't allowed in here.
They might find out how depressing
it is to be an adult.
```

Send   Print

Mm Medicine Cabinets

RapidTransmit from DariaM

Isn't "ointment" a cool word?

Send
Print

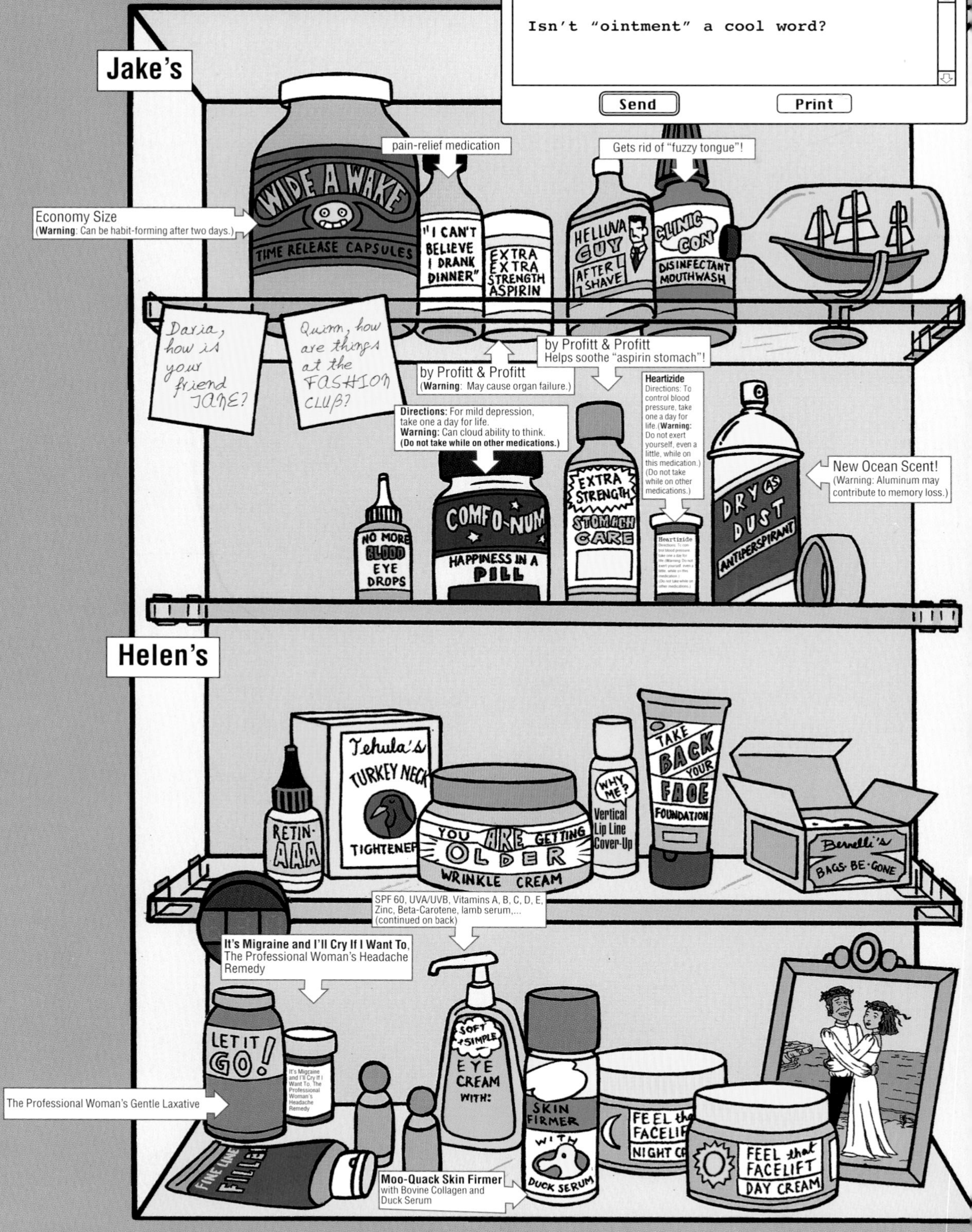

Jake's
WIDE A WAKE
TIME RELEASE CAPSULES
Economy Size
(**Warning**: Can be habit-forming after two days.)
pain-relief medication
"I CAN'T BELIEVE I DRANK DINNER"
EXTRA EXTRA STRENGTH ASPIRIN
Gets rid of "fuzzy tongue"!
HELLUVA GUY AFTER SHAVE
CLINIC CON DISINFECTANT MOUTHWASH
Daria, how is your friend JAKE?
Quinn, how are things at the FASHION CLUB?
by Profitt & Profitt
(**Warning**: May cause organ failure.)
by Profitt & Profitt
Helps soothe "aspirin stomach"!
Heartizide
Directions: To control blood pressure, take one a day for life.(**Warning:** Do not exert yourself, even a little, while on this medication.) (Do not take while on other medications.)
Directions: For mild depression, take one a day for life.
Warning: Can cloud ability to think.
(Do not take while on other medications.)
NO MORE BLOOD EYE DROPS
COMFO-NUM HAPPINESS IN A PILL
EXTRA STRENGTH STOMACH CARE
Heartizide
DRY AS DUST ANTIPERSPIRANT
New Ocean Scent!
(Warning: Aluminum may contribute to memory loss.)
Helen's
Tehula's TURKEY NECK TIGHTENER
RETIN-AAA
YOU ARE GETTING OLDER WRINKLE CREAM
WHY ME? Vertical Lip Line Cover-Up
TAKE BACK YOUR FACE FOUNDATION
Bernelli's BAGS-BE-GONE
SPF 60, UVA/UVB, Vitamins A, B, C, D, E, Zinc, Beta-Carotene, lamb serum,... (continued on back)
It's Migraine and I'll Cry If I Want To,
The Professional Woman's Headache Remedy
LET IT GO!
It's Migraine and I'll Cry If I Want To. The Professional Woman's Headache Remedy
The Professional Woman's Gentle Laxative
SOFT & SIMPLE EYE CREAM WITH:
SKIN FIRMER WITH DUCK SERUM
FEEL that FACELIFT NIGHT CREAM
FEEL that FACELIFT DAY CREAM
FINE LINE FILLER
Moo-Quack Skin Firmer
with Bovine Collagen and Duck Serum

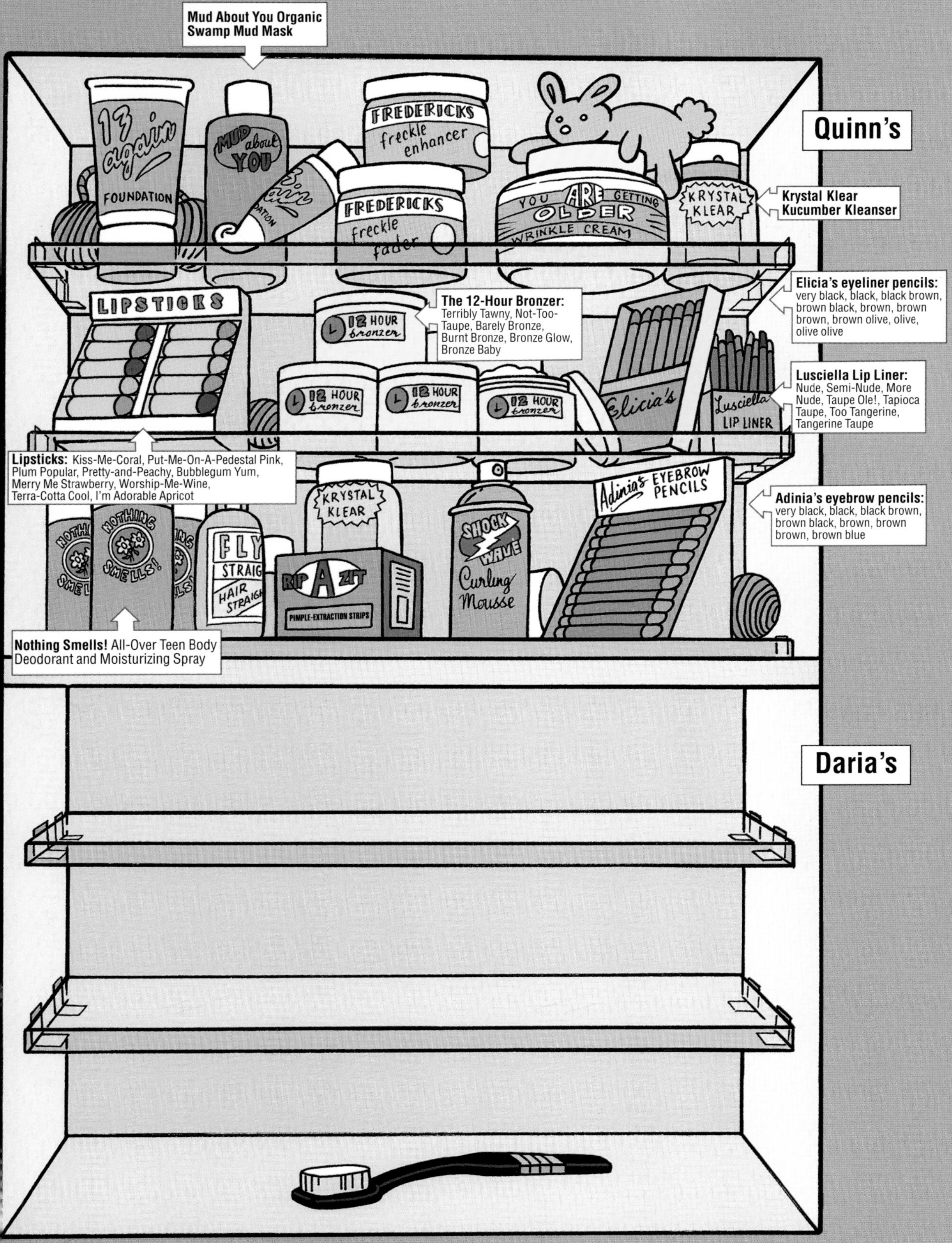
Mud About You Organic Swamp Mud Mask
Quinn's
13 again FOUNDATION
MUD about YOU
FREDERICKS freckle enhancer
FREDERICKS freckle fader
YOU ARE GETTING OLDER WRINKLE CREAM
KRYSTAL KLEAR
Krystal Klear Kucumber Kleanser
LIPSTICKS
The 12-Hour Bronzer: Terribly Tawny, Not-Too-Taupe, Barely Bronze, Burnt Bronze, Bronze Glow, Bronze Baby
12 HOUR bronzer
Elicia's
Elicia's eyeliner pencils: very black, black, black brown, brown black, brown, brown brown, brown olive, olive, olive olive
Lusciella LIP LINER
Lusciella Lip Liner: Nude, Semi-Nude, More Nude, Taupe Ole!, Tapioca Taupe, Too Tangerine, Tangerine Taupe
Lipsticks: Kiss-Me-Coral, Put-Me-On-A-Pedestal Pink, Plum Popular, Pretty-and-Peachy, Bubblegum Yum, Merry Me Strawberry, Worship-Me-Wine, Terra-Cotta Cool, I'm Adorable Apricot
NOTHING SMELLS!
KRYSTAL KLEAR
SHOCK WAVE Curling Mousse
Adinia's EYEBROW PENCILS
Adinia's eyebrow pencils: very black, black, black brown, brown black, brown, brown brown, brown blue
RIP A ZIT PIMPLE-EXTRACTION STRIPS
Nothing Smells! All-Over Teen Body Deodorant and Moisturizing Spray
Daria's

Nn New Year's Resolutions

Jake

Learn the names of Quinn's friends.

Learn the name of Daria's friend.

Put the romance back in our marriage and stop faking like I'm asleep.

Not let that punk at the racetrack talk back to me anymore.

Let go of the fact that my father was a cold, spiteful man who sent me off to military school at a ripe and tender age and thereby ruined my life. No point in dwelling on it!

QUINN'S QUIPS 'n' QUOTES

I will try to add more bounce to my walk.

I will finish inventorying those darn scrunchies!!!

I will learn to accept the fact that other people are just jealous of me.

I will be a better friend to Stacy so I can find out what Sandi's saying behind my back.

I will try to tan more evenly.

VITALE, DAVIS, HOROWITZ, RIORDAN, SCHRECTER, SCHRECTER, AND SCHRECTER
ATTORNEYS-AT-LAW

Helen

Schedule more quality time with Daria and Quinn.

Schedule more "intimate" time with Jake (before he falls asleep).

Schedule more phone time with Mom.

Schedule more time to "just relax."

Increase billable hours by 30 percent.

LAWNDALE LIONS

PAIN IS PASSING. PRIDE IS PERMANENT.

Mack

I will get Kevin to stop calling me "Mack Daddy" if it kills me.

Next time Kevin wants to demonstrate how to stop a brick with his head, I'll let him.

I will not show Ms. Barch fear, no matter what she does to me.

I will stop fantasizing about tricking Brittany into jumping out a window.

I won't let it bother me that Jodie puts student council, homework, tennis club, French club, the debate team, and just about every other damn thing ahead of me.

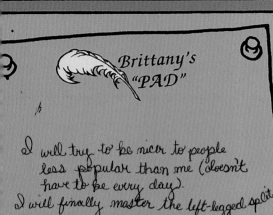

Brittany's "PAD"

I will try to be nicer to people less popular than me (doesn't have to be every day).
I will finally master the left-legged split.
I will expand my vocabulary by learning a new word every month.
I will figure out those self-adhesive stamps.
I will continue teaching Kevin to be a gentleman. A lot of progress last year!!!

BEEFY BURGERS.

KEVIN
MY NEW YEAR'S
REZOL, RESSOU,
RESULLATIN, RESLLUTI
OH, FORGET IT!

Jodie Abigail Landon

I will volunteer at the soup kitchen.
I will learn Sanskrit.
I will take a papermaking class.
I will become a crossing guard.
I will do anything to get out of the house so Dad will leave me alone about my grades and friends and what colleges I'm going to apply to and agggh!

Daria

Stop wearing heart on sleeve.
Master level 20 of CyberKron.
Cut back on whirlwind social schedule.
Grow further apart from Quinn.
Shake up my routine: Order sausage instead of pepperoni.

RapidTransmit from DariaM

"Happy New Year" is a contradiction in terms.

Send   Print

Oo Oration, Kevin's and Mack's

LAWNDALE LIONS

PAIN IS PASSING. PRIDE IS PERMANENT.

MEMO

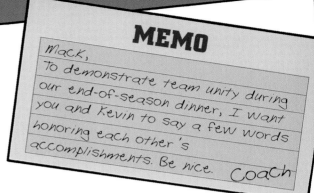

Mack,
To demonstrate team unity during our end-of-season dinner, I want you and Kevin to say a few words honoring each other's accomplishments. Be nice. Coach

I'd like to begin by thanking the Young Executives of Lawndale for sponsoring the Thirty-Third Annual Lawndale Lions' End-of-Season Dinner. Your unwavering support means a lot to us, and thanks for all the "Lawndale Means Business!" helmet decals.

I'd like to say a few words honoring our star quarterback, Kevin Thompson. Kevin is...our quarterback. To be a great QB, you need outstanding physical skills, an intricate knowledge of the game and, above all, the ability to inspire your team to fight to the finish, even when all appears lost. ~~And Kevin...~~

Take John Elway. At 37, people said his glory days were over. Yet last winter he galvanized his team and, against all odds, took the Broncos to their first Super Bowl victory in Colorado history.

The Lawndale Lions have won many games with Kevin as their quarterback. ~~Kevin is best known for his unabashed ability to take credit for things he had nothing to do~~ Another great quarterback is Brett Favre. Ten years younger than Elway, Favre is arguably the best passer in the league. The Olympian efforts of these two great athletes made Super Bowl XXX the most exciting game in decades. Kevin...saw the game.

When I think back on all the great QBs-Joe Montana, Joe Namath, Brett, John-I realize they have one quality in common: A dynamite charisma that says: "This guy's a winner, and as long as we've got him, we're in the game." Kevin...never mind

Coach, do I have to do this?

LAWNDALE LIONS

PAIN IS PASSING. PRIDE IS PERMANENT.

COOL HELMET STICKERS! THANKS. I'M GONNA TALK ABOUT OUR TEAM CAPTAIN, MACK DADDY! BUT MY DAD SAYS ALWAYS START A SPEECH WITH A JOKE, SO HERE GOES. A BLIND GUY GOES INTO A DEPARTMENT STORE WITH HIS BLIND PERSON'S DOG. HE PICKS UP THE DOG AND STARTS SPINNING IT AROUND. THE SALESLADY WALKS UP TO HIM AND SAYS, "WHAT ARE YOU DOING?" AND HE SAYS: "JUST SPINNING MY DOG AROUND." (SAVE TIME FOR LAUGHS.)

MACK DADDY IS A REALLY GOOD TEAM CAPTAIN. OF COURSE, THE QB, THAT'S ME, IS REALLY THE LEADER OF THE TEAM. I'M THE ONE THE BALL GETS HIKED TO AND WHO CALLS OUT THE PLAYS. AND I GET ALL THE BABES. HA, HA, JUST KIDDING. ACTUALLY THE QB USUALLY DOES GET MORE BABES THAN THE CAPTAIN. AND A LOT MORE BABES THAN THE LINEBACKERS—NO OFFENSE, GUYS.

BEING TEAM CAPTAIN ISN'T EASY. AT LEAST I DON'T THINK IT'S EASY. MAYBE IT IS EASY. I DON'T KNOW. BUT I'M SURE MACK DADDY CAN HANDLE IT. YO MACK DADDY!

MY DAD SAYS ALWAYS LEAVE THEM LAUGHING, SO IN COLLUSION, A SNAIL DIES AND GOES TO HEAVEN. THIS GUY NAMED PETER TELLS THE SNAIL HE CAN HAVE ANYTHING HE WANTS. THE SNAIL ASKS FOR A RACE CAR, AND PETER PUTS AN "S" ON IT SO THE SNAIL KNOWS IT'S HIS. ONE DAY, THE SNAIL IS RACING AROUND, AND ONE ANGEL TURNS TO THE OTHER AND SAYS "WOW! LOOK AT THAT S-CAR DRIVE!"

THANKS!

RapidTransmit from DariaM

Thinking. Writing. Reading. Public speaking involves all the things Kevin does best.

Send   Print

Pp Pep Talk, Mr. O'Neill's, Drama Horizons

From the desk of
TIMOTHY O'NEILL

Wow. Just look at you in your marvelous costumes. I am so proud today to be gazing upon my budding thespians—and I'd like to express a few heartfelt words before we venture forth onstage.

Many of you have worked very hard for this, some harder than others, but this is no time for finger-pointing—unless to say, "You! YOU'RE doing a great job!" And as you bask in the glory of this evening's limelight, I want you to do more than just SPEAK your lines. I want you to BECOME your character.

So, Quinn, hard as it may be, I'm asking you to dig deep inside, deep, deep inside, and TRY to put yourself in poor, sweet Emily's position. Imagine the agony and the torment of knowing that two NOBLE knights in shining armor are desperately in love with you but, in vying for your affections, only one man can win—in a fight to the death! Oh, the anguish, the guilt you would feel!

And Kevin, I want you to…if you could just remember which scene you're in, Kevin, that would be great.

Remember, too, that all actors, from Alan Alda to Shelley Winters, had to start somewhere. So when you're out there underneath the glare of the bright lights, think of this as more than just a high school play with all your friends and family watching: think of this as that first hurdle to winning international acclaim for your acting. And maybe one day, in your Oscar acceptance speech—don't laugh, you've got the talent!—perhaps you'll recall this night fondly and maybe even think to mention how our modest little Drama Horizons was a big turning point in your life. Naturally, should that magical day occur, I trust you will not engage in any untoward speculation about people's lifestyle orientation. It's not true, anyway.

Now I want everyone to take a minute and visualize the audience. As we finish our wonderful play, they finish their delicious dinner and leap up as one in a standing ovation. Brava! Brava! Yum! Yum! And now let's bow our heads for a moment and remember poor James Dean.

Okay, everyone! Have a great show!

RapidTransmit from DariaM

Now go out there and show them why people make fun of school plays!

Send Print

Pp Political Acumen

LAWNDALE HIGH SCHOOL

HIGH SECURITY FOR HIGH PERFORMA

VOTE
BUSH
2000

The Honorable George W. Bush, Governor
The State House
Austin, Texas

Dear Governor Bush,

It is a rare occasion indeed when I write to a public official, but in this particular instance I felt I could hold back no longer.

Since you took office in 1995, 59 condemned men have gone to their deaths. Not once did you commute or delay a death sentence, despite numerous pleas from the ACLU, Amnesty International, and other rights organizations. Nor did you show clemency for the first woman to be executed in Texas since 1863, even though Pope John Paul II himself intervened. Your state leads the country in total executions by a large margin, having hit a record high of 37 in 1997. All I can say to you, Governor Bush, is: Keep up the good work!

Saving taxpayer dollars by refusing to send pickax murderers off to a cushy life in jail with TV and a weight room is commendable. And to those who criticize the way you run your state, I ask this: If it's such a bad place, why then are hundreds of foreigners trying to sneak in every night? You don't find that happening in liberal Massachusetts, that's for sure!

You know, your governorship, as a high school principal I believe our jobs are not that different. I currently spend 80 percent of my school operating budget on surveillance cameras, Dobermans, spot locker checks and occasional strip searches just to ensure every child his or her constitutional right to a safe and free education. Yet I wonder if my efforts would be even more effectual if I could somehow drive home the consequences of veering off the straight and narrow.

I think you may know where this is going, your excellency. If we are going to employ the death penalty as a deterrent, why limit ourselves to murder? I have already written to the Governor of Utah about securing Gary Gilmore's electric chair. I know that the apparatus on which Karla Faye Tucker was executed is probably not available, because you are no doubt still using it (to which I say, huzzah!). I was hoping, however, that I could visit Huntsville to take photographs from which I could have a duplicate made. By prominently displaying these items in the school's entrance hall, I hope to provide students with a stern reminder of what awaits them should they cut a class, fail to use a No. 2 pencil, or otherwise start down the long road to a squandered, felonious life.

I hope you can see your way toward granting my request. As a "thank you" in advance, I'd like to offer my suggestion for a campaign slogan should you decide to seek higher office: "Déjà Vu All Over Again—Bush for President in 2000!" Catchy, no?

Once again, keep up the good work. Perhaps when I'm in Huntsville we could meet over coffee. I'd love to get your take on the gratuitous banning of assault weapons.

Respectfully yours,

Angela Li

Ms. Angela Li
Principal

RapidTransmit from DariaM

`Next thing you know, they'll be letting jaywalkers off with life.`

Send | Print

Qq Quinn's Essay

ACADEMIC IMPRISONMENT
by Quinn Morgendorffer

No light shines through these four brick walls. For the school is my prison, and its teachers my imprisoners. Like a hamster on one of those wheel things, school runs us around and around until we yearn for the little food pellet—but only more homework awaits.

Is school not in fact a form of discrimination against teens? For there are no laws that say adults have to go to school. And why not? Because adults made these laws and then passed another law saying we couldn't vote and take back their laws! And so we are kept from the malls all day, only to get there in the afternoon when they're really crowded and we have to wait in long, long lines for the dressing rooms. The kind of lines that form at the dessert counter during lunchtime...IN PRISON!

Yes, we're like prisoners, forced to break rocks in the hot sun without sunscreen nor lip balm. Why is ours the sole land where school is mandatory? In other nations, children have the freedom to get a job in the clothing industry or whatever. Why are we not allowed the same liberties? No, we must learn to add and divide even though the world has tons of accountants. We must learn to spell, even though we have spell-check. And all this history stuff. Who cares? It's over! (Although I like those gowns that French queen wore—the headless one.)

So go ahead! Lock me up with your homework and your tests! Rob my freedom with your reading and your thinking. As far as I'm concerned, the only difference between school and prison is the wardrobe. Or do you want to take away my outfits, too?

The End

RapidTransmit from DariaM

I've got to give Quinn credit for trying. My patience.

Send Print

Qq Quinn's Excuses for Breaking Dates

RapidTransmit from DariaM

When Quinn really puts her mind to something... there's going to be trouble.

Send   Print

DATE/GUY	EVENT	REASON/EXCUSE	REACTION	NOTES
11/11 Steve	Dance	C.O./"I forgot Chad asked me first."	"But my mother was going to lend me her BMW."	Made sure Chad was still taking his Dad's Porsche.
11/12 Chad	Dance	C.O./"I forgot Michael asked me first."	"But I made reservations at Chez Pierre before the dance."	Told him he could take me to Chez Pierre, and then I'd meet Michael afterward.
11/12 Michael	Dance	C.O./"I forgot Jonathan asked me first."	"But that's the same thing you told Chad."	Told him I can't possibly remember everything and if he was going to have that attitude, then just forget it.
11/13 Spencer	Chez Pierre	S.W./"I have to study."	Said if I didn't want to go out with him, then just say so, instead of making up ridiculous excuses.	Next time use a believable excuse.
11/14 Brad	Chez Pierre	C.O./"I thought you said WEDNESDAY night."	Apologized and agreed to Wednesday.	Since Brad is cuter than Mark, reschedule Mark from Wednesday to next week.
11/15 David	Dinner & Movie	C.O./"Mom's making the family have dinner with her before she leaves for Aunt Ellie's funeral."	"That's what you said last month."	Check excuse logs more thoroughly in future.
11/16 Keith	Mother's wedding	O./Said I was grounded.	Said he couldn't bear to go to the wedding alone and couldn't I be grounded next week? I said teenage discipline doesn't work that way.	Someone told him (probably Sandi!) that Jay and I went to Slippery SlideWorld; avoid for a week.
11/16 David	Chez Pierre	S.S./"Something's come up."	He said "What?" I said I couldn't remember, but it was very important. He tried to reschedule. I said I'd get back to him.	He asked Sandi out, and she said yes, so she was just saying she wouldn't go out with him so I wouldn't go out with him. Next time get a second opinion from Tiffany.

Code: C.O. - Cuter Offer   S.S. - Sandi said SHE wouldn't go out with him
S.W. - Found out Staci went out with him   O. - Other

Quinn-
Le Cosmetique called—your colors are in
Quinn-
Stacy called
Quinn-
Sandi called-
says call her before calling Stacy back
Quinn-
Tiffany called-
couldn't understand but had something to do with Sandi
Quinn-
Call Joey
Quinn
Call Corey
Quinn-
Call Jeffy
Quinn-
Call Jared, I mean Jamie
Quinn-
Call Sean
Quinn-
Call Brett
Quinn-
Call Matthew
Dammit, Quinn!
ON YA!!
LODGE
EAT YA PIZZA
Vitale, Davis, Horowitz, Riordan, Schrecter, Schrecter, and Schrecter
Attorneys-at-Law
Sorry girls—Business dinner—Lasagna in fridge
Daria—Tell Mr. O'Neill I can't make parent/teacher conference. Can I send Marianne?
Quinn—Can't make mother/daughter spa day
Can I send temp?
Jake—Can't make it to the counseling office. I'll try to conference call
JAKE MORGENDORFFER
CONSULTING
"we consult!"
Lawndale High Spring
RAFFLE
Win a State-of-the-Art Home Security System
NO. 357
NO. 358
NO. 359
NO. 360
NO. 361
YES!

RapidTransmit from DariaM
Communicating via the refrigerator just isn't the same as face-to-face conversation. It's better.
Send
Print
Birthday Present Suggestions!
1. Mauve leather coat with faux-fur trim
2. Yacht Party for 100 with cute plastic monkeys in drinks
3. Convertible (I'll keep in garage till I'm old enough, I promise!)
4. Walk-In Closet (could get extra space from Daria's room)
5. Still can't decide? I'm registered at Cashman's!
COMA CALM
DEPARTMENT OF MOTOR VEHICLES
SUSPENSION
5 MINUTE GOURMET
NOTICE OF VIOLATION
SPEEDING
Jake Morgendorffer
CK-TIE GALA FOR:
AGAINST AID
THE END OF COMMUNICATION: REFRIGERATOR NOTES AND THE DISINTEGRATION OF COMMUNICATION IN THE AMERICAN FAMILY
BY DARIA MORGENDORFFER
A+
You've obviously done your research!
DEAR DARIA MORGENDORFFER,
YOU HAVE WON 2 FREE COPIES OF
SPORTS FIEND MAGAZINE
50 GREATEST PUNTS VIDEO

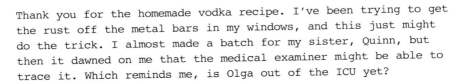

DariaM, 3:34 AM, Re: 1

From: DariaM
Date: 12/12
To: Borisborscht@minskuniv.org
Subject:

Dear Boris,

Thank you for the homemade vodka recipe. I've been trying to get the rust off the metal bars in my windows, and this just might do the trick. I almost made a batch for my sister, Quinn, but then it dawned on me that the medical examiner might be able to trace it. Which reminds me, is Olga out of the ICU yet?

In answer to your question, I don't find dating in this country stressful at all, probably because I don't do it. My mother thinks I'd have a better social life if my provocative style of dress didn't advertise the fact that I'm only after one thing: Isolation. I certainly don't get this new fad of people falling in love and getting engaged on the Web before they've ever met. It would make much more sense to me to marry someone and THEN interact with them only through e-mail.

I guess what I'm trying to say is that as generous as your offer was to put yourself up in my room for a month, I'm afraid I'll have to decline, as that would fall under the category of human contact. My sister, on the other hand, might be interested in meeting you when you come to visit this fall. Just tell her your Russian accent is French (she thinks the French are really cool because they invented French dressing), and you'll be all set.

Daria

RapidTransmit from DariaM

I started my own Cold War at home, but no one noticed anything different.

Send Print

Ss School Activities

Daria,
And what's wrong with one of *these* clubs?
Mom

LAWNDALE HIGH SCHOOL

HIGH SECURITY FOR HIGH PERFORMANCE.

Memo:

To: All Students
From: Jodie Landon, Student Council Vice President

Extracurriculars Still Available!

Just to let you guys know, the following clubs are still accepting new members, but you'd better sign up now before they're all filled up.

Archery Club — Only if I can practice in the living room.

Band — Good idea. Now I can realize my dream of marching in public dressed as a Christmas tree ornament.

Debate Team — Involves taking sides.

Drama Club — Requires facial expressions.

Fencing Club — Okay. But that wimpy protector tip comes off my foil before dueling.

Glee Club — Only if you promise to come to all my recitals.

Hiking Club — Requires use of legs.

The Pom-Pom Girls — Yes, I've always wanted to go to college in Aruba.

Spanish Club — No hablo.

Tennis Club — Requires exposure to the outdoors.

Young Optimists — Mom, did you let your prescription lapse again?

RapidTransmit from DariaM

School activities are for people who haven't discovered the thrill of counting ceiling cracks.

Send | Print

Ss Sexual Harassment

SEXUAL
HARASSMENT

LAWNDALE HIGH SCHOO

HIGH SECURITY FOR HIGH PERFORMAN

TO: All Female Faculty and Students
FROM: Ms. Janet Barch
RE: Sexual Harassment Has Happened to You!

The beginning (or end or middle) of a new marking period is always a good time to renew our vigilance against Sexual Harassment. If you are under the impression that this problem is confined only to the halls of government, corporations, the armed forces, small business, nonprofit organizations, international diplomacy, high technology, world finance and space exploration—wake up, sister! ALL men, by nature of their sex and total moral bankruptcy, live to debase women. No female is safe from these equal-opportunity defilers, for they care not of their victim's race, socioeconomic background, or past experiences with ex-husbands who desert them after twenty-two years of unconditional servitude, dammit!

Women have been tyrannized for so long that many of us now think such vile treatment is normal, even acceptable. So inured are we to this oppression perpetrated upon us by the abusing sex that we habitually miss the cues that are indeed the hallmarks of demeaning sexual harassment.

To delineate between normal interaction and molestation, I have compiled a brief list of things to watch out for. Should any of these behaviors sound even remotely familiar, report to me immediately so we can pursue legal action.

In School:
- Did he LOOK at you?
- Did he sit NEXT to you?
- Did he TOUCH you inappropriately in any way? Your shoulder, your arm, your hand as you, say, unsuspectingly passed back the tests?
- Did he hold the door open for you so he could ogle your buttocks as you walked by?
- Did he ask you for the time—i.e., get you to stand still so he could mentally undress you?
- Did he make lewd comments such as "nice coat" as in, "Why don't you take off your coat, hop into bed, and make me breakfast before you leave in the morning?"

On a Date:
Dating opens another can of worms and is best avoided until you're thirty, if then. But if you are coerced into one, here's what to sue for:
- At the movie, did he take the aisle seat so he could keep you from leaving?
- Did he buy you popcorn so he could lewdly watch you lick the butter from your lips?
- Did he say you looked nice—in other words, "Nice rack! Woo-hoo!"
- Did he insist on picking you up in his car so he could "accidentally" brush his lecherous hand against your knee as he shifted out of park?
- Did he pay for dinner, as in, "Now that I spent $10.99 on this lousy meal it's time for you to throw away your pride and submit to me so I can have something to brag about to my equally depraved and women-hating friends?"
- Did he walk you to your door and try to force his no-good, two-timing, wife-deserting, freeloading body upon you under the guise of a good-night kiss, and did you tell him to leave you the hell alone, dammit, you see right through his empty promises and cheap, tawdry designer shirts, and he'll never—do you hear me? Never!—suck you dry of all your dignity and lifeblood and whatever else he can take again! Never! Never! Never!

Elsewhere:
- Was he breathing?

RapidTransmit from DariaM

Ms. Barch believes that all men are beasts, and vice versa.

Send | Print

Ss Sick, Sad World, Stringer Guidelines

Dear Budding Reporter,

Thank you for your inquiry and congratulations on your extraordinary timing. SICK, SAD WORLD is currently accepting story "pitches" from freelance reporters. Experience is not necessary--all that's required is a desire to work hard and a hunger for something like the truth!

We're interested in brief, entertaining, news-resembling stories that you won't see anywhere else. Our viewers are busy, vibrant people--they don't have time to sit through a lot of boring facts and big words. We rely on snappy copy and eye-catching visuals to keep our show part of their lively lifestyle. Don't worry if you can't completely back up your story with facts--we have producers for that. Just make sure any idea you pitch elicits a gut reaction of "That's sick!" The categories we're most responsive to are:

1. Human interest--Baby Born with Artificial Leg; Tree Grows in Stomach of Lemonade Drinker; Space Aliens Living in "Pagodas" (that's Martian for "house"!)
2. Medical science gone awry--My Face-lift Came Off in My Hands!; Leper Reduced to Stump; Doctor Grows Human Hearts in Cabbage Patch
3. Common household threats--Can Drinking Drain Cleaner Cause Alzheimer's? Our Experts Find Out; Decorative Trim Kills Family of Three; When Faucets Attack!
4. Arts & Crafts you can make at home--Shoelace Vests, Fur-Ball Coats, Peach-Pit Earrings and Other Fine Gifts
5. Homicidal anything
6. Cute animal stories--Cats Who Stalk; Peeping Tom Pit Bulls; Eye-Gouging Pigeons
7. Newsbreaking events--"Ho, ho, ew!"--Goosing Santa Caught on Tape; Toilet-Paper Thief Strikes Roadside Bathrooms; Psychics Accused of Cheating in Soda Taste Challenge
8. Cannibal grandparents

The best way to approach SICK, SAD WORLD is to fax us as many story ideas as possible. (Don't forget to include the phone numbers for sources you plan to use.) The more ideas the merrier. Keep in mind that stringers tend to submit similar stories, so don't be surprised if you see something you pitched on the air. We didn't rip you off. Another reporter just beat you to the punch and, besides, we have a large staff of full-time lawyers.

SICK, SAD WORLD retains the rights to alter any or all portions of your story for entertainment purposes. You'll also be asked to sign a standard waiver absolving us of any lawsuits and/or capital crimes that may result from the airing of your story.

In the event we decide that we like your pitch, we will contact you; there's no need to try to track down our unlisted phone number. If you haven't heard back from us within a week of your fax, feel free to send more ideas until you hit the jackpot. Remember, if at first you don't succeed, try, try again!

Good luck!

SICK, SAD WORLD EDITORIAL STAFF

RapidTransmit from DariaM

Truth may be stranger than fiction, but a good bear attack gets better ratings than either.

Send Print

Tt The Three J's Quinn Central, Reconnaissance Room

LAWNDALE HIGH
ASHMAN'S
QUINN'S HOUSE
KEY
MOST COMMONLY USED ROUTE.
MOST COMMON ALTERNATIVE
ROUTE USED TO DITCH THAT WEIRD COUSIN OF HERS.
·QUINN'S SCHEDULE·

08:45–09:00
Arrives at South Door

09:00–09:50
(Room 101)
Earth Science

09:50–09:57
First-Floor Girls' Bathroom

10:00–10:50
(Room 206)
Math Strivers

10:50–10:57
Second-Floor Girls' Bathroom

11:00–11:50
(Room 212)
History Through Film

11:50–12:22
Second-Floor Girls' Bathroom

12:25–12:47
Cafeteria

12:49–12:57
First-Floor Girls' Bathroom

01:00–01:50
Poetry of Sixties Music

RapidTransmit from DariaM

Hey, I think I see something... oops, sorry, it's just my last shred of dignity.

Send Print

RED PHONE: Unlisted number for Quinn's use only. The line is to be kept clear at all times in case she calls. It has yet to ring.

1. Sunglasses Quinn borrowed from Jeffy and accidentally stepped on
2. Rearview mirror from Jamie's BMW yanked off by Quinn when checking eyeliner
3. Scrunchy Quinn discarded after the elastic gave out
QUINN'S FAVORITES
Chip: Ridged
Crackers: Square
Pretzels: Twisty
Ice: Crushed
Soda: Brown, diet
Straw: Bendable
Garnish: Teensy-weensy lemon slice
Animal: Bunny, because they're so cute when they eat lettuce
Color: Pink, but deep pinkish instead of white pinkish
Books: Decorative
Movies: No action, subtitles, or stories based on books
Presents: Lots
4. Pencil Quinn borrowed from Joey and then chewed up
5. Portable CD player Quinn borrowed from Jamie and inadvertently dropped four floors
COMPUTER: Quinn screen saver
BLACK PHONE: To report Quinn sightings. Phone mainly used by Jamie to throw Jeffy and Joey off Quinn's trail, as in, "She's right here at Cashman's, hurry!"
WASTEBASKET:
Picture of Jamie and Quinn at the Skee-Ball Park, secretly torn up by Jeffy.
Picture of Joey and Quinn at Chez Pierre, secretly torn up by both Jamie and Jeffy.
Picture of Jeffy and Quinn shoe shopping at Cashman's, secretly torn up by Jamie.

Tt Time Capsule, Lawndale High

Memo:

To: All Faculty and Students
From: Angela Li, Principal
Subject: Time Capsule

Lawndale High is currently constructing a time vault, so that in the event of mankind's annihilation in a nuclear holocaust, future civilizations, or perhaps archaeologists from another planet, will be able to unearth this capsule and get a glimpse of what life was like around the turn of the century, 2000 A.D.

I am asking everyone to donate one item and your explanation of why it says something significant about our times. Participation is not mandatory, but those who fail to contribute will not be allowed to graduate. I will be the judge of what is and is not suitable for inclusion. If you have any questions regarding my decisions, please feel free to see me so that we may discuss and dismiss your arguments in a prompt and expedient manner.

Thank you for contributing to the spirit of Lawndale High.

Mr. DeMartino: **A knife and salt shaker.** "These items represent the total net worth of the average American teacher."

Mack: **A photo of Kevin.** "Do not let descendants near heavy machinery."

Kevin: **Tape of a Lawndale Lions game.** "So you guys have something to watch in case the video stores are closed! And, hey, I'm the QB!"

Jane: **Sculpture of an alien with plaque reading: Miton, King of the Earth, 1999.** "Our leader."

Ms. Li: **Fingerprint powder.** "This is how we identified felons and class cutters. I wish I could see the DNA stamping you future people use now!"

Brittany: **Good Luck chain letter.** "Sorry! I needed to send out one more letter so I wouldn't break the chain!"

Fashion Club: **Blow dryer.** "To help with Armageddon Hair."

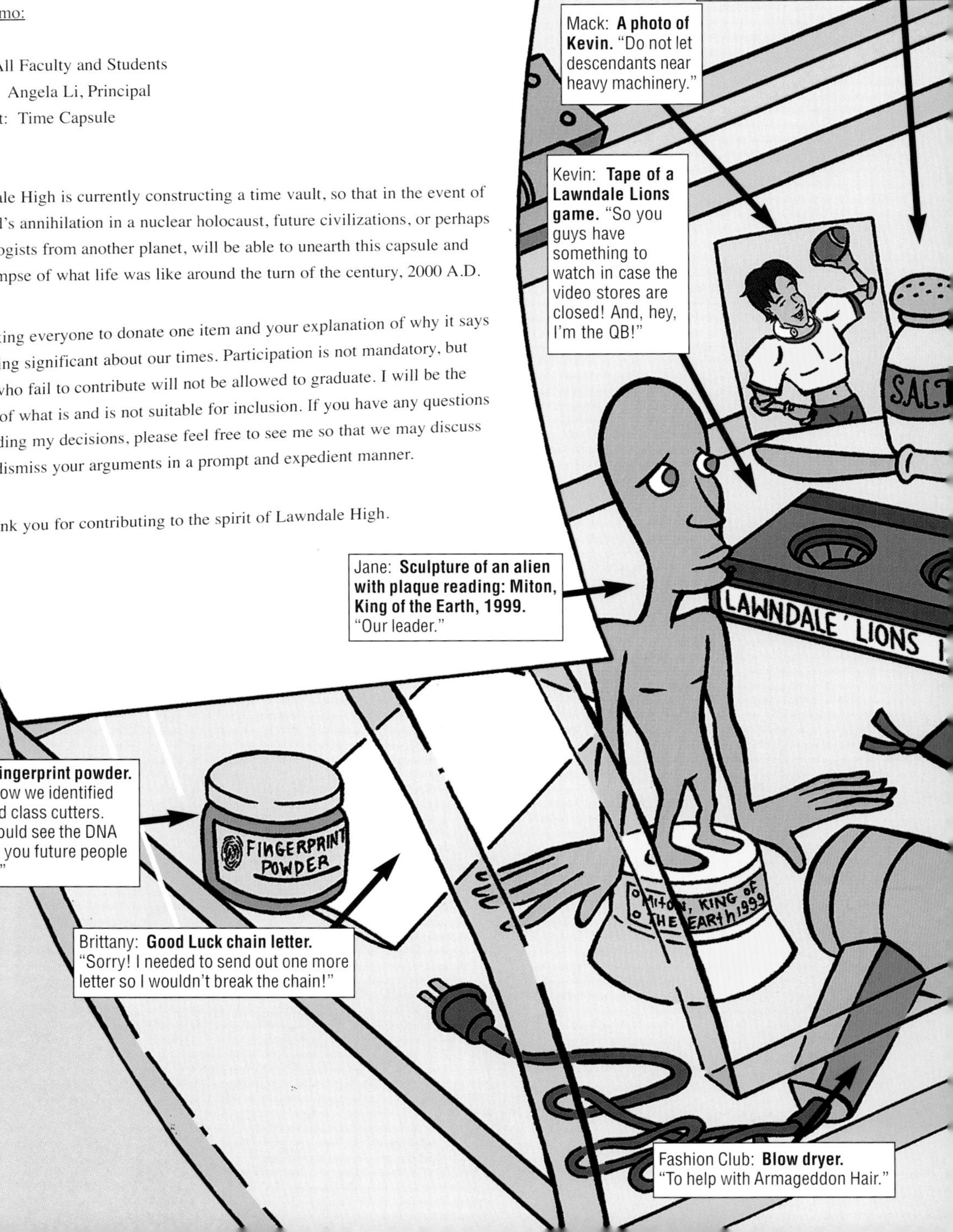
SALT
LAWNDALE' LIONS
FINGERPRINT POWDER
MITON, KING OF THE EARTH 1999

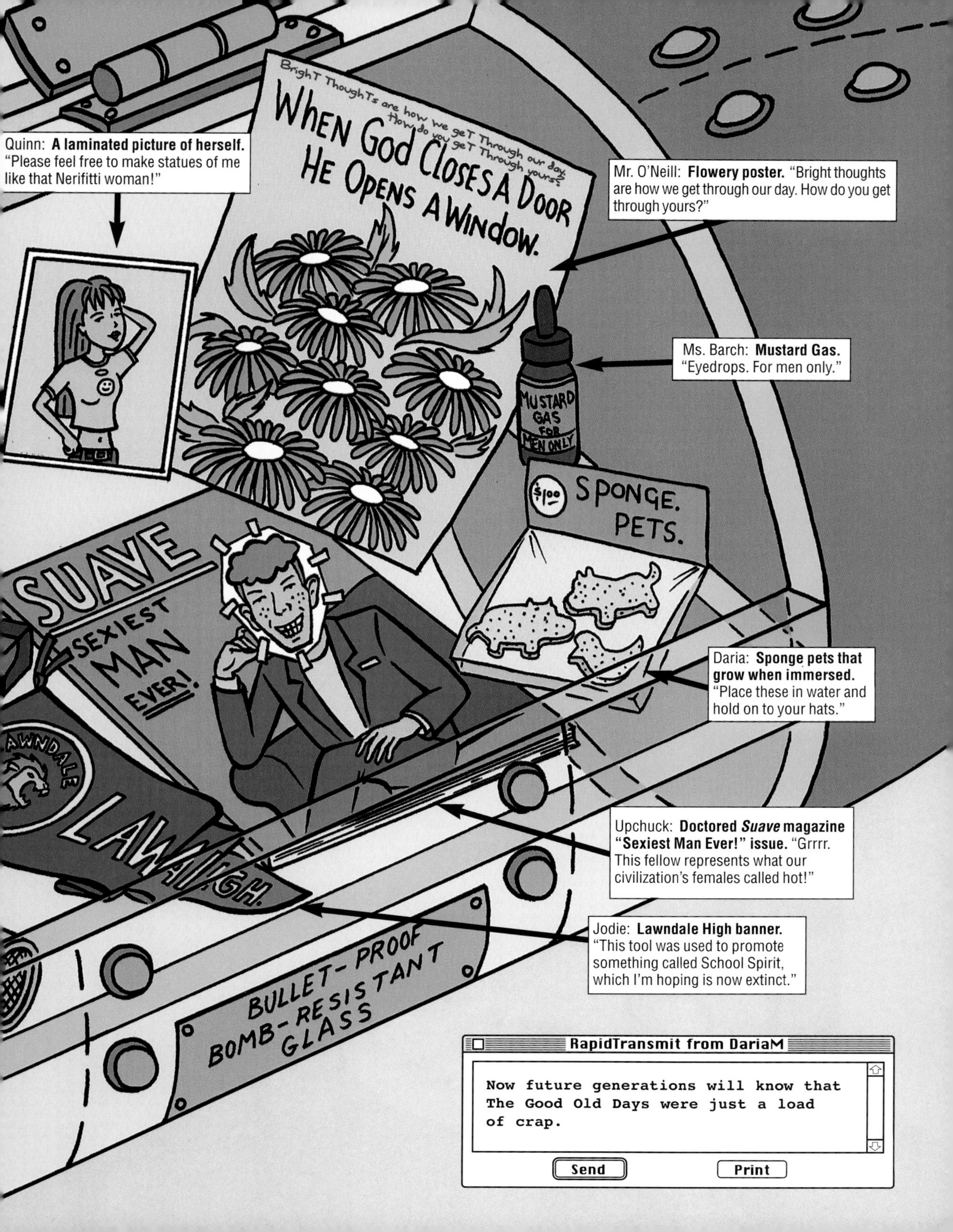
Bright Thoughts are how we get Through our day. How do you get Through yours?
When God Closes A Door He Opens A Window.
Quinn: **A laminated picture of herself.** "Please feel free to make statues of me like that Nerifitti woman!"
Mr. O'Neill: **Flowery poster.** "Bright thoughts are how we get through our day. How do you get through yours?"
MUSTARD GAS FOR MEN ONLY
Ms. Barch: **Mustard Gas.** "Eyedrops. For men only."
$1.00 SPONGE. PETS.
SUAVE SEXIEST MAN EVER!
Daria: **Sponge pets that grow when immersed.** "Place these in water and hold on to your hats."
LAWNDALE LAWNDALE HIGH.
Upchuck: **Doctored *Suave* magazine "Sexiest Man Ever!" issue.** "Grrrr. This fellow represents what our civilization's females called hot!"
Jodie: **Lawndale High banner.** "This tool was used to promote something called School Spirit, which I'm hoping is now extinct."
BULLET-PROOF BOMB-RESISTANT GLASS
RapidTransmit from DariaM
Now future generations will know that The Good Old Days were just a load of crap.
Send
Print

Uu Under the Beds, Jane's & Trent's

Jane's Bed

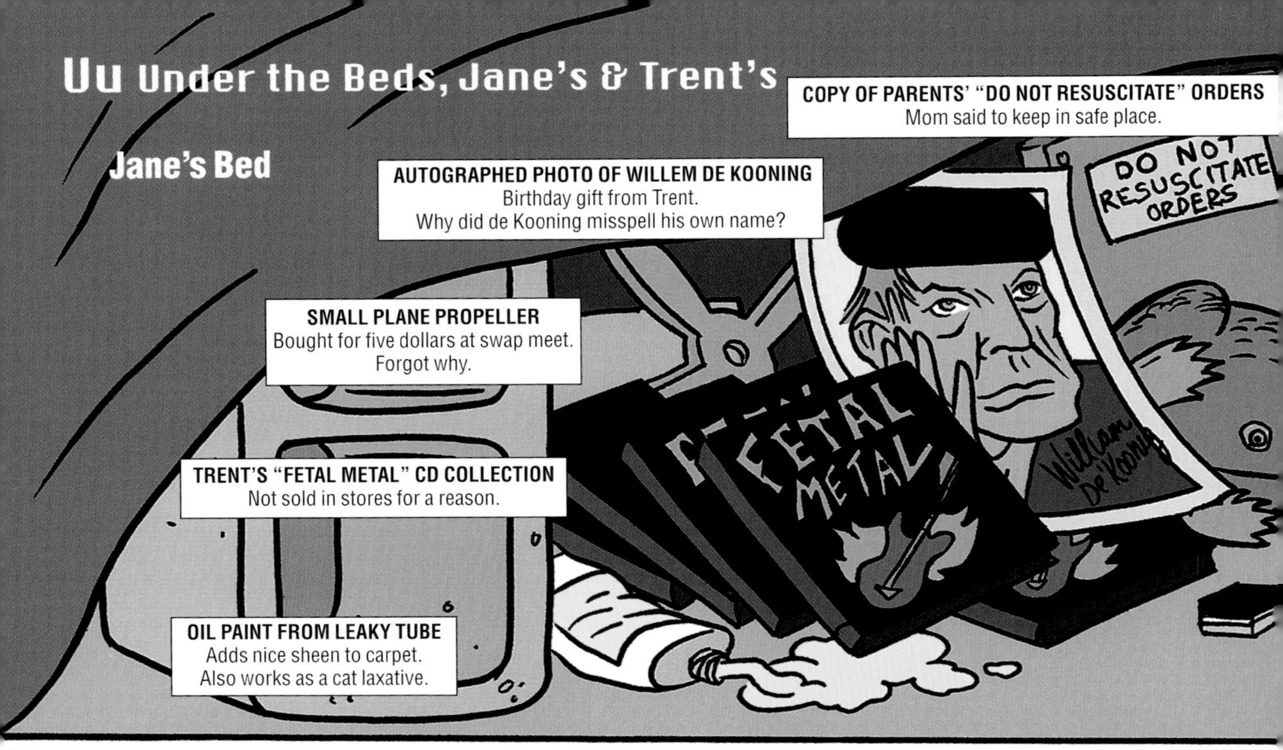

COPY OF PARENTS' "DO NOT RESUSCITATE" ORDERS
Mom said to keep in safe place.
DO NOT RESUSCITATE ORDERS
AUTOGRAPHED PHOTO OF WILLEM DE KOONING
Birthday gift from Trent.
Why did de Kooning misspell his own name?
William De Kooning
SMALL PLANE PROPELLER
Bought for five dollars at swap meet.
Forgot why.
TRENT'S "FETAL METAL" CD COLLECTION
Not sold in stores for a reason.
FETAL METAL
OIL PAINT FROM LEAKY TUBE
Adds nice sheen to carpet.
Also works as a cat laxative.

Trent's Bed

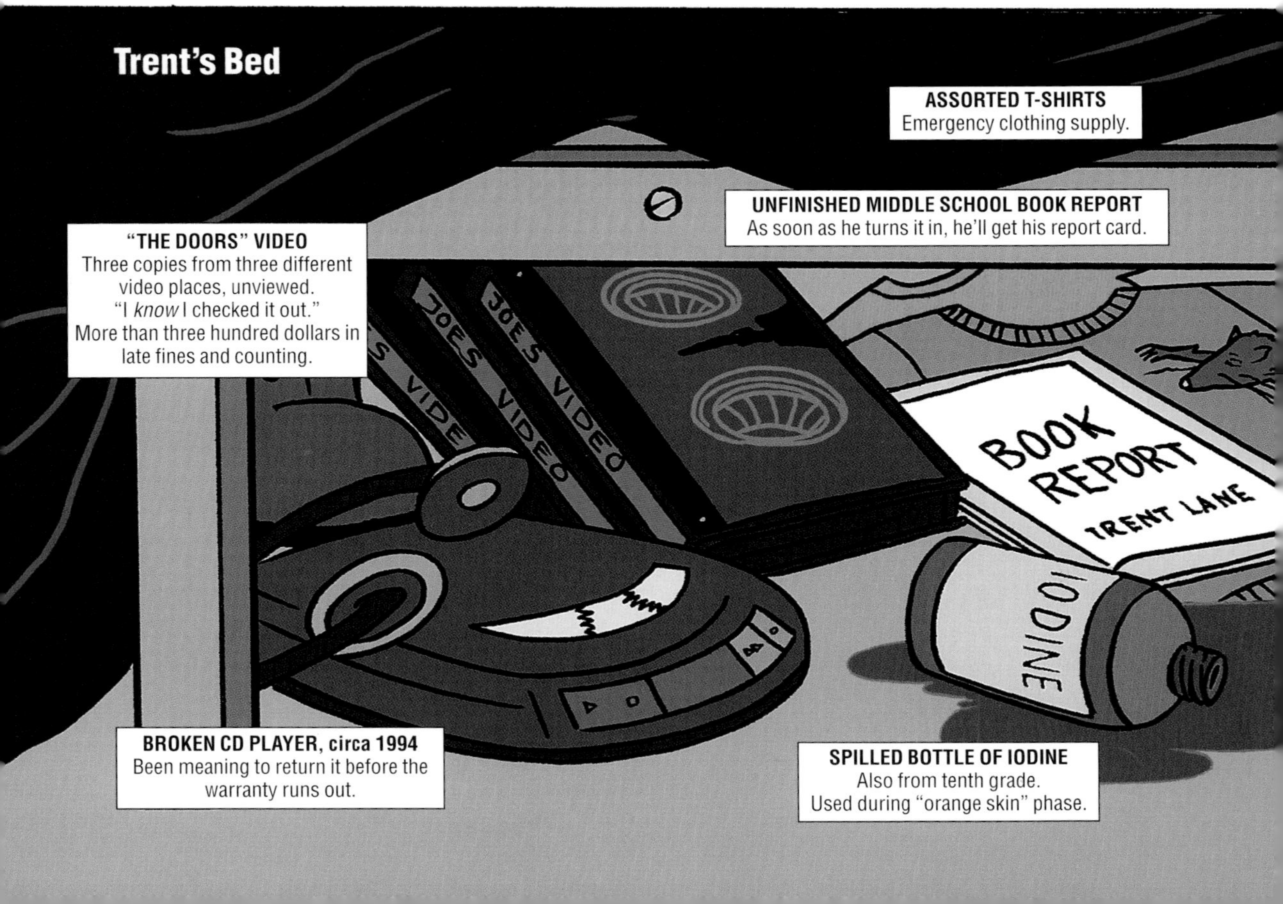

ASSORTED T-SHIRTS
Emergency clothing supply.
UNFINISHED MIDDLE SCHOOL BOOK REPORT
As soon as he turns it in, he'll get his report card.
"THE DOORS" VIDEO
Three copies from three different video places, unviewed.
"I *know* I checked it out."
More than three hundred dollars in late fines and counting.
JOES VIDEO
JOES VIDEO
BOOK REPORT
TRENT LANE
IODINE
BROKEN CD PLAYER, circa 1994
Been meaning to return it before the warranty runs out.
SPILLED BOTTLE OF IODINE
Also from tenth grade.
Used during "orange skin" phase.

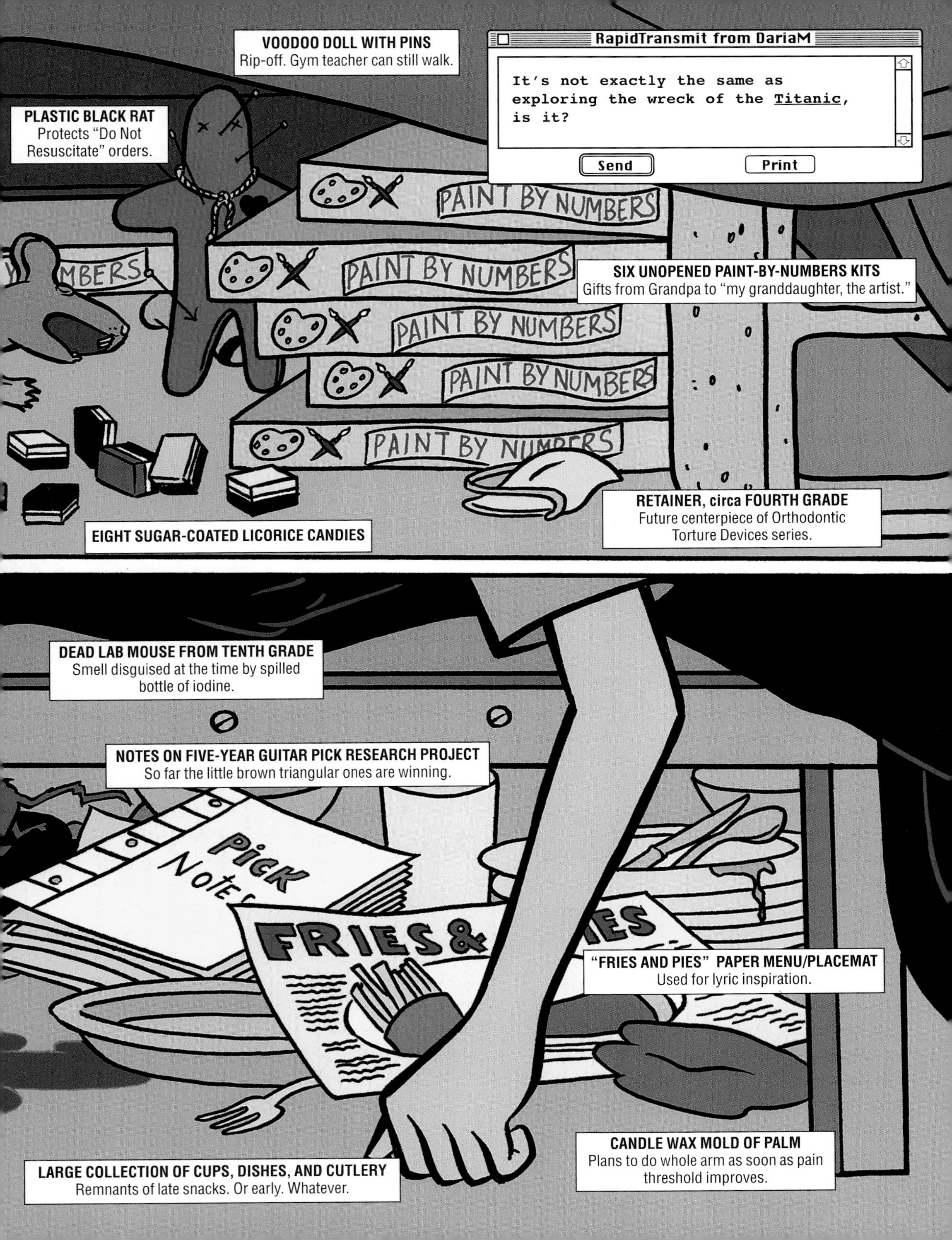

VOODOO DOLL WITH PINS
Rip-off. Gym teacher can still walk.
RapidTransmit from DariaM
It's not exactly the same as exploring the wreck of the Titanic, is it?
Send
Print
PLASTIC BLACK RAT
Protects "Do Not Resuscitate" orders.
PAINT BY NUMBERS
SIX UNOPENED PAINT-BY-NUMBERS KITS
Gifts from Grandpa to "my granddaughter, the artist."
RETAINER, circa FOURTH GRADE
Future centerpiece of Orthodontic Torture Devices series.
EIGHT SUGAR-COATED LICORICE CANDIES
DEAD LAB MOUSE FROM TENTH GRADE
Smell disguised at the time by spilled bottle of iodine.
NOTES ON FIVE-YEAR GUITAR PICK RESEARCH PROJECT
So far the little brown triangular ones are winning.
Pick
"FRIES AND PIES" PAPER MENU/PLACEMAT
Used for lyric inspiration.
CANDLE WAX MOLD OF PALM
Plans to do whole arm as soon as pain threshold improves.
LARGE COLLECTION OF CUPS, DISHES, AND CUTLERY
Remnants of late snacks. Or early. Whatever.

Uu Unique Sculptures, Jane's

WHILE SCULPTING ISN'T QUITE THE SAME AS HAVING YOUR HANDS AROUND SOMEONE'S NECK, AT LEAST IT'S A START.

Uu Upchuck's "The Rules for Dating Feisty Chicks"

Charles Ruttheimer III

Mr. Michael Perry, Publisher
Tomcat Books
1222 Avenue of the Americas
New York, New York 10020

Dear Mr. Perry:

Allow me to introduce myself. I am Charles Ruttheimer III, and my reputation for conquering members of the fairer sex is—dare I say it?—legendary. So often do my fellow males turn to me for advice in the art of amore that I cannot answer all their questions and still have time for the ladies. It therefore occurred to me that my secrets of seduction would make a guaranteed best-seller. Consequently I have put together a brief sampling of the book I have in mind for your consideration. Enjoy!

<u>Chapter 4: The Rules for Seducing Feisty Chicks at Parties</u>

Rule #1: **Dress the part.** Feisty chicks love men with a certain *je ne sais quoi*. I myself prefer to don an ever-so-silky satin tuxedo jacket, an ascot and an ornamental pipe. As one feisty female complimented through her luscious lips upon viewing my ensemble: "Oh, look, honey. They let Hugh Hefner out for a walk."

Rule #2: **Make her come to you.** When you walk into a crowded room, gently brush up against your object de amore, give her a little "grrrrrr" (tips on how to "grrrrr" will be covered in Chapter 16), and cross to the opposite side of the room. Each time you catch her eye, look at her longingly, and ever so gently purse your lips. Chances are she won't be the only foxy lady to notice.

Rule #3: **If she doesn't come to you.** Many femmes fatale like to play hard to get. Others could be intimidated by your ultrasuaveness or by the flock of long-legged lovelies already hanging on your every word. Put her pretty mind to rest. Slowly saunter over, give her a moment to take in the sensual swirl of your pheromones, and then sweetly whisper in her ear: "Your life has just begun." Then all you have to do is stand back. Stand pretty far back, just in case she has an adverse reaction to so much concentrated masculinity. You might also want to shield any vulnerable areas on your body.

Rule #4: **Don't take it personally if you are asked to leave.** This often occurs when a male is throwing the shindig and is jealous of all the attention the ladies are lavishing upon you. If the party-giver is a gal, she could be hurt that you chose not to vie for her affections—ah! A woman scorned, I know her so well. Simply exit without incident and tell your latest love interest that you'll be waiting for her outside, after the party, in rapt anticipation. It's a good idea to conceal a folding chair in the bushes before the party begins, so that once you have been thrown out you won't have to stand during what could be a wait of several hours.

Well, Mr. Perry, what do you think? If love has a biographer, I am that scribe. I look forward to hearing from you!

Your new best-selling author,

Charles Ruttheimer III

RapidTransmit from DariaM

Other guys love Upchuck because he makes them look so good.

Send   Print

Vv Vice Presidential Duties, Fashion Club

Quinn, here are those job descriptions I wrote. Give me your honest, honest opinion, vice president to president.

Love, Sandi

Fashion Club Job Descriptions

President

Responsible for deciding on topics for weekly meetings (Python Espadrilles: Fad or Bad?), determining community-service projects (like teaching Robin Leonard how to tweeze her unsightly eyebrows, like what was she thinking anyway?) and rejecting prospective members. Must look really good in everything and have a perfectly symmetrical face. Absolute authority to call an emergency shopping expedition anytime, day or night. All presidential decisions are to be considered final unless perhaps you think you can do a better job?

Currently held by Sandi

Vice President

Largely ceremonial. Responsibilities include writing reports on trends (even ugly ones, like smiley-face nail decals) and compiling the Fashion Club Hall of Shame list (designers who make clothes in fat-people sizes, models who think that just because they make a million dollars a year they can get away with baggy jeans in public, etc.). Also responsible for taking pictures of fashion disasters for monthly group discussions. Must be ready to assume presidential duties in the event that president receives million-dollar modeling contract. Until that happens, take orders like you're supposed to. Even skin tone required.

Currently held by Quinn

Coordinating Officer

Responsible for compiling three-day fashion-forecast chart of each member so we don't wear the same thing to school or clash. Also responsible for updating Color Schemes of Restaurants list so we don't, say, wear red when sitting in a red booth and thus risk "fading" into the decor, although, if you're really well put together, that shouldn't be a problem. Must score at least 95 percent on Mix and Match test.

Currently held by Tiffany

Secretary

Responsibilities include keeping the minutes of all meetings and making sure there are lots of diet sodas, carrots, and celery on hand. Neat penmanship a must. And stop freaking out every time you see a bug.

Currently held by Stacy

Sandi, this is really, really good! But shouldn't you put in something about the vice president taking over if the president gets maimed or disfigured or something? Not that I could ever hope to fill your shoes! But not because they're especially big or anything. Um, you know what I mean.

Love, Quinn

RapidTransmit from DariaM

Upon confiscating this document, the enemy rejoiced--for they knew the brain-eating spores had worked.

Send | Print

Fashion Magazine Spreads for Weekly Debates

Discuss: Fad or Bad?

Can big lips make your nose look smaller?

Crude or Prude?

When sunglasses make you look smart.

Fashion Disaster Alert:

Doesn't she know opaque stockings make ankles look thick?

Like, what's with all the earrings? And they're not even dangly!

Oh, please. That thing on her hand looks like something out of Mid-Evil times.

Ww "While We're Away..."
Housekeeping Notes from the Lanes

Dear Janie and Trent,
Sorry we didn't have a chance to say good-bye before we left this evening, but you guys were still asleep. Anyway, we're off on our tour of Eastern European hamlets—we did tell you we were going, right?
Here's a list of things you need to do while we're away:
If the electricity goes off, check the lamp i[n] the den, the one with the chewed up electrica[l] cord (darn cats). Your father says it can cause shorts. Otherwise, call the electric company. I think we paid the bill, but I'm not sure. If we forgot, give them the check I signed and fill in the amount. (We've left behind a bunch of blank checks, so just use them as things get shut off.)
There may be some food left in the refrigerator, or check the freezer. FYI: Dad tried to thaw out his sneakers last night and found out the oven isn't working. Does anyone remember the last time we used it? In any case, if you need to heat up food in the kiln, nothing drippy, okay?
The roof in our bedroom leaks so if it rains, make sure you change the buckets. I don't want the floor to warp any more than it already has. Dad tried tarping the roof with a trash bag, but, you know. Dad.

SUGAR
RapidTransmit from DariaM
This list would have been very helpful if the Lanes had remembered to leave it home.
Send
Print
Remember to feed Zachary and Taylor. I tried to find them before we left, but you know how cats are. Their food is in the cupboard, or by the litter box, or check the freezer. And PLEASE change their litter this time. The health inspector isn't going to be so forgiving if he has to come back for a repeat visit. The plumber is stopping by sometime this week to fix the drain in the bathroom sink. If he finds my brass pendant from Monterey Pop down there, I definitely want it back. Mother may come for a visit. You know what she looks like.
MESSAGE FOR YOU!
The washing machine is clogged. (Another lump of clay—sorry.)
Please record The Mister Fixer-Upper Handyman's Show. (You know how Dad can be if he misses an episode.) I left behind a bunch of tapes, I think.
I thought I heard voices coming from the basement last night, so it's possible that those squatters from last summer are back. I'm pretty sure they're harmless, but you might want to call the police if they bother you. Make sure it's not one of your brothers or sisters or their kids before you call the cops.
Please water any plants that are still alive.
I forgot to cancel my Women in Clay support group, so they'll still be coming over. Don't serve them any beverages with caffeine, tannin or sulfites.
The garbage should be taken out at some point. I think the garbage cans are by the garage somewhere.
If you have any questions or an emergency comes up, wire us in Albania at—I'll call you as soon as I find the number.
And please—no parties! I don't want to find the house a mess when we get back.
Love, MOM

Xx Xanadu — Professional Couples Counseling

Jake, here's another copy of the questionnaire. It's my last one, so this time _please_ try to keep your temper, okay? Love you—H

XANADU • PROFESSIONAL COUPLES COUNSELING •

Dear Married Professionals,

Do you find yourself avoiding intimacy by running off to meetings or burying your head in the paper? Have you stopped budgeting sex into your schedule? Do you ever look at your husband or wife and think: "What is this person doing in my house?"

Yes, couples often grow apart, and, in fact, many greet this process with considerable relief. But marital strain can affect job performance, which in turn can knock you right off the fast track at the office—so your marriage is worth saving! And at Xanadu Professional Couples Counseling, we've got the objective data-gathering intrasystem and interpersonal relationary management skills to have you cuddling again in no time.

Just fill out this simple questionnaire, and send it back with your $400 nonrefundable consultation fee (this may be a reimbursable expense; check with your accounting or human resources department). Based on your answers, we will determine your specific needs and tailor a treatment program specially designed to bring you and your loved one closer together. Do it today!

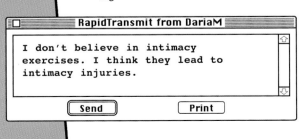

RapidTransmit from DariaM

```
I don't believe in intimacy
exercises. I think they lead to
intimacy injuries.
```

Send | Print

XANADU
COMPATIBILITY QUESTIONNAIRE

Instructions: Questionnaires are to be filled out separately. Do not show your answers to your spouse.

1. How long have you been married?
A. 1 to 10 years
B. 10 to 15 years
C. Over 15 years
D. Is it me, or is time slowing down?

2. Were you married before?
A. Yes
B. No
C. Like I would do this twice

3. How many children do you have?
A. 1
B. 2 or more
C. I will, I swear! Just not now.

4. Our children say we:
A. Still act like newlyweds
B. Act like an old married couple
C. Need a vacation
D. Aren't fooling anyone

5. When you first met, what most attracted you to her/him?
A. Intelligence
B. Appearance
C. Sense of humor
D. Family business

6. What attracts you now?
A. The same qualities as before
B. His/her phenomenal success
C. His/her unconditional love
D. The Australian Outback

7. My spouse's eyes are:
A. Green
B. Blue
C. Brown
D. Wait. I know this one.

8. When my spouse enters the room I:
A. Hear my heart go pitty-pat
B. Know that I am looking at my best friend
C. Make a business call to Tokyo
D. Fake like I'm dead

9. How often do you have sexual relations?
A. At least once a week
B. At least once a month
C. At least once a year
D. Define "sexual relations"

10. I wish my husband/wife were:
A. More romantic
B. More successful
C. More nurturing
D. Missing

11. My idea of a romantic evening is:
A. A walk on the beach
B. A bottle of wine in front of the fireplace
C. Dinner for two at a French restaurant if I can write it off
D. Excuse me, is this going to take long?

12. To get our marriage back on track, we should:
A. Discuss our feelings more openly
B. Increase our hours at the office
C. Take a second honeymoon
D. Take separate honeymoons

13. I wish we had more time to:
A. Share activities together
B. Talk and snuggle
C. Catch up on work
D. Date other people

14. The last time my spouse told me he/she loved me was:
A. This morning
B. Last week
C. Over the Internet
D. During the Bush Administration

15. If I could do it all over again, I would:
A. Marry the same partner
B. Pursue the same career path
C. Start my family earlier
D. That's it. Just twist the knife a little deeper.

Yy Yearbook

To Sir/Ma'am With Love—

YES I CAN!

Later on, some of the students will wonder why they dreamed about *The Old Man and the Sea*.

Mr. D assures the class that "there are no stupid questions. Just stupid people."

RapidTransmit from DariaM

I love learning. I just wish school weren't always in the way.

Send Print

The Special Bond Between Teachers and Students

UDY HALL
I am male, therefore I suck
I am male, therefore

Ms. Barch helps a student with his self-esteem.

D-TECT A THIEF

"After the test, those No. 2 pencils are to be *returned*!"

Hang in there!

Mrs. Manson tries to remember what today's hot lunch is.

Ms. Defoe reassures a student that you don't have to draw to be a car model.

Thanks to recent advances in medical treatment, paramedics were able to save some of the gym class.

TEACHERS LOUNGE

The best thing about teaching is that you get back as much as you give.

Zz Zimbabwe, E-mail to

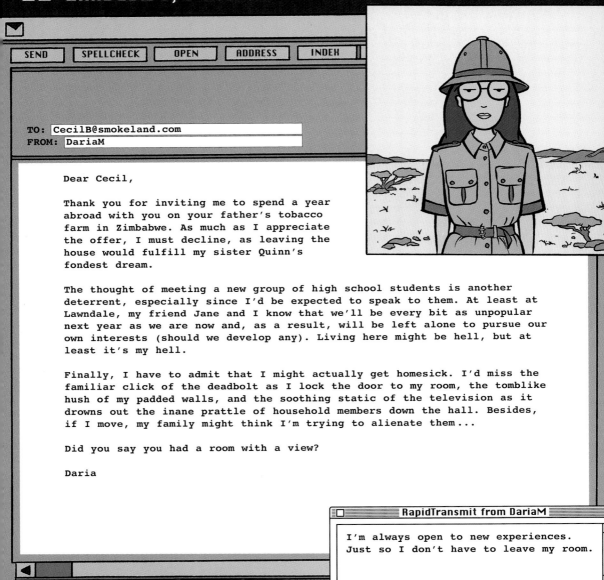

SEND | SPELLCHECK | OPEN | ADDRESS | INDEX

TO: CecilB@smokeland.com
FROM: DariaM

Dear Cecil,

Thank you for inviting me to spend a year abroad with you on your father's tobacco farm in Zimbabwe. As much as I appreciate the offer, I must decline, as leaving the house would fulfill my sister Quinn's fondest dream.

The thought of meeting a new group of high school students is another deterrent, especially since I'd be expected to speak to them. At least at Lawndale, my friend Jane and I know that we'll be every bit as unpopular next year as we are now and, as a result, will be left alone to pursue our own interests (should we develop any). Living here might be hell, but at least it's my hell.

Finally, I have to admit that I might actually get homesick. I'd miss the familiar click of the deadbolt as I lock the door to my room, the tomblike hush of my padded walls, and the soothing static of the television as it drowns out the inane prattle of household members down the hall. Besides, if I move, my family might think I'm trying to alienate them...

Did you say you had a room with a view?

Daria

RapidTransmit from DariaM

I'm always open to new experiences. Just so I don't have to leave my room.

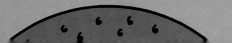

Send | Print